How to

Think Like a Millionaire and Get Rich

How to

Think Like a Millionaire and Get Rich

by
Howard E. Hill

Parker Publishing Company, Inc.
West Nyack, N.Y.

PRINTED IN THE UNITED STATES OF AMERICA

B & P

Dedicated to
my wife
Edith Ives Hill

What This Book Will Do
for You

The fifteen fundamental truths which you are about to learn can be put to work this very day, with powerful results. All you have to do is apply a finger-tip push of *resolve* to your thinking and you are on your way to undreamed-of success. It might take a day or a month, but the abundance that will be yours is surely worth the small amount of effort required.

When you have all the supporting information you will need in order to begin thinking like a millionaire, you will be ready to organize your findings into a realistic plan of action. In your quest for facts you will discover that so basic are the principles of increase that any person—man or woman—with a spark of drive can make the step-by-step plan work on demand.

Before you progress very far in your quest for riches you will make the surprising discovery that thinking like a millionaire and becoming one possess some rather startling parallels. You will find, moreover, that the thought almost without exception precedes the accomplishment.

Perhaps some persons who invoke these fifteen principles of growth in the exact order as given, even in full force and absolute quality, will not become instant millionaires simply by willing it so, but there is one quite surprising fact that emerges with amazing clarity. Any man or woman who puts this program of increase in motion will be greatly enriched in money, mind, and achievement.

You can begin now with the first forward step and each day add a new million-dollar advantage to your present way of life. The only limitation you will find in this amazingly easy program of increase is the need to develop certain sustaining qualities in order to hang on to your wealth once it has been acquired.

Why not give all fifteen steps an honest and determined try? You will not only be thinking like a millionaire—you will *be* one before too long.

Contents

The Sixth Step to Riches

How to Strike It Rich with a Bank Account of Contacts

How to Use Three Golden Words. How to Put the Idea in Action. How to Reap the Rewards of Time and Patience. Where to Find Four More Golden Keys. How to Activate the Five Dynamics That Will Attract and Hold Contacts. How to Find Money Value in Contacts.

The Seventh Step to Riches

How to Build a Name Power That Attracts Success

The Basic Qualities of "Name Power." Planned Name Building. Positive Image Building Techniques. When to Do Something "On Spec." Nineteen Dynamic Ways to Build "Name Power." You Can Be Your Own "Image Builder." The Knack of Getting Things Done. Find Your Niche and Settle Down Comfortably.

The Eighth Step to Riches

Why Creating a Personality Plus Helps You to Think Like a Millionaire

Why Intensity is the Measure of Desire. How to Activate the Ten Sustaining Pillars of a Powerful and Magnetic Personality. The Search for New Experiences. How to Jockey for Position. Try Opening a New Door Every Day. You Can Move with the Tides of Fortune. How Long Is Enough? A Rolling Stone Gathers Money. Intensity Is the Measure of Desire. Ten Sustaining Pillars of a Powerful and Magnetic Personality.

How to

Think Like a Millionaire and Get Rich

*The First Step
to Riches*

How to Make the Law of Accrual
Work for You

Within each and every one of us there is a spark of genius. All that is needed to fan this tiny flame into an inferno of action is strong, affirmative desire. This can be achieved by a very neat and easily operated plan.

To begin thinking like a millionaire, all you have to do is sit still long enough to determine one basic fact about yourself. It is, *What makes me tick?* In other words, what urge, drive, or interest motivates you? It is as simple as that.

The Fire Power That Builds Success

When you have isolated the mental spur that goads you into action, you have found the *propellent* which will boost you into the millionaire orbit, regardless of whether the purpose that gets you out of the two-bit rut and into the favored circle of millionaires is sex, success, recognition, or promotion. The all-clear signal at this point is *go . . . Go . . . GO!*

With the word that touches off the *fire-power* within

you well in mind, decide exactly what it is you want to possess, accomplish, or gain and then write it out, clearly and briefly. Let us say, for example, that you have written, "I want to be a millionaire."

The very first step you take is to make a personal inventory—and for Pete's sake, don't let this direction throw you. What I am going to suggest is not a preachment, but a ray of enlightenment. In the first place, you have certain attributes, natural tendencies, talents, inclinations, some formal education, mixed with at least a foundation of experience values. List them, and be quite certain that you enter them in your stock of personal advantages as *assets*—never as a brake or drag on what you are about to accomplish. Remember the wise old Chinese philosopher who said, "A journey of a thousand miles begins with a single step."

Now that you have listed all of the favorable items in your background, count your cash on hand. The important point to keep in mind from this moment on is that this is your capital account: *it cannot be touched for any reason whatsoever.* Here we come to the catch in this overly-simplified plan of action. This capital account must be increased each and every day, even if it is only by *one penny*.

The Habit of Daily Growth

Oddly enough, this apparently ingenuous act of daily growth is the seed from which great fortunes spring. It serves to create the thoughts or thinking that nurture millionaires. It is precisely as the prophet Job wrote (chapter 22, verse 28): "Thou shalt also decree a thing, and it shall be established unto thee. . . ."

When you have prepared the indicated groundwork for thinking like a millionaire, you are ready for the final all-important step. To think like a person of great wealth, you must keep that "carrot" or goal constantly in mind, as well as the daily addition of substance that spells an increase in your fortune—*and* you must take one more forward step.

Start With a Mental Cleansing

Since it is now quite generally agreed that all health, wealth, and outstanding success originates in the mind, it stands to reason that this seeding ground for great fortunes must be cleansed of all that is unworthy. This concept isn't a pipe dream artfully devised by some pseudo-psychologist; it is established as a scientific fact based upon the experience of literally thousands of men and women who have earned a million dollars and at the same time developed one essential skill—the ability to hang on to their money.

Begin today to eliminate from your thinking habits all negative thoughts: all regrets, hates, resentments, superstitions, and/or fears. In other words, rid your mind of any thoughts or attitudes of defeatism. *I am going to win:* this is your constantly-affirmed declaration from this moment on.

"Them As Has, Gets"

This homely colloquialism probably erupted from the depths of overwhelming frustration; nevertheless, it expresses a profound truth. It is known that whenever a determined man or woman adds something to his or her possessions, what has been acquired will tend to attract an increase. What the advantage will be is often difficult to predict, but of one thing you can be certain; *something will be added to you.*

How or with what you enlarge your holdings is irrelevant. I once knew a young man who hungered to own land, although at the time he was eking a bare existence as a thirty-dollar-a-month farm hand. One day, in desperation, he took an abandoned wooden crate and filled it with soil and declared, "This land is mine. Some day it will include all of this valley." This chap took his small "plot" of earth to the bunkhouse and shoved it under the crude lumber frame that served him as a bed. Each day he would pull the crate from under his bunk and repeat with great intensity the affirmation that he had made in the beginning.

The rough itinerant workers who shared this youngster's ramshackle quarters joshed him unmercifully about his "property," but he stuck to his purpose. It wasn't long until the story about the boy who was "tetched in the head" about owning land filtered into the nearby town. But there were two persons who didn't laugh. One was a girl, daughter of the livery stable owner, and the other was a disillusioned farmer, Jake Snowden, who had homesteaded a hundred and sixty acres of land when the valley was first opened to settlers. Late one Saturday afternoon he met the boy in the general store and, more in jest than anything else, said, "Son, give me twenty dollars and you can have my deed to the Sandy Corners place." Without a moment's hesitation the boy counted out twenty dollars, all the money he had in the world and replied, "I'll take it."

With this meager start, the boy kept on buying distressed land at bargain prices, until one day he owned over a thousand acres of marginal farm property. In the meantime he married the girl who liked what she saw, and today his sons manage the ranch while he and his wife travel wherever fancy takes them.

"Picturing" Can Make Your Dreams Come True

The lesson here is obvious. If you want something badly enough, all you have to do is start now with whatever is available, even if it is only a picture of what you want to possess.

If the idea of growing with pictures eludes you, listen to this: John Gaddes was a young man with some ambition, and he wanted to own a Cadillac convertible. Although he kept his jalopy polished and tuned to the full extent of its potential, he just wasn't satisfied. One day he picked up a copy of a current magazine in which the gleaming jewel of a car—the exact image of his dreams—sparkled in all the available elegance of the lithographer's art. This was exactly what he wanted. Clipping out the picture, he neatly folded it for his wallet, and several times each day he would take it out and drool over its shiny brightness, little realizing that he was energizing a power of natural law that would not be denied.

One day a friend mentioned that his father-in-law could no longer drive the family Cadillac. Would John be interested, for a price? He was. Within hours he had the carefully tended two-door sedan in his possession, for a ridiculously small sum of money. Disposing of the jalopy was no problem: an eager high school student grabbed it for almost as much as he had paid for the "Cad." With this much of a start, John kept right on picturing the car of his dreams.

Learn to Take One Step At a Time

John was scarcely acquainted with his new possession when he was able to trade up for a later model in even better condition, and all of this apparently without any effort on his part. Actually, however, he had set in motion a basic law of increase when he visualized with intensity precisely what he wanted to possess. Best of all, he had to assume only a very small obligation with the bank in order to reach his goal.

Big Deals Grow From Little Idea Seeds

This might come as a surprise to most persons, but a high percentage of big money-making deals started with very commonplace ideas. The trick is to build the ordinary brain child into something special. There are many ways to accomplish this purpose. In order to get you on the right track, here are the five basic patterns for your use. You will then be able to take your pick of the plan or stratagem that best serves your purpose, or you might want to combine one or more of the methods. Or better yet, with a flash of imagination, this may supply a new twist that will blast you overnight into the stimulating atmosphere of the comfortably wealthy.

1. Take a commonplace idea and by adding a dash of color, a new twist, or an unusual name or use, win great acclaim, and perhaps a fortune.

2. Make it a resolute habit to add something to your idea each and every day. The unceasing practice of daily growth is irresistible.

3. Make the law of accrual or attraction work for you by picturing, or possessing, a fractional part of what you want to achieve.

4. Find where the action is. That is, learn who might be interested in the type of idea you have in mind.

5. Once you have found the idea you want to develop, put real go-power into your new interest and fire it with enthusiasm. From this point on, nothing can stop you.

It sometimes happens that ideas reach the explosive stage as if they were triggered by an atomic blast. The reason for this is obvious. Humanity responds to the unusual in a most fantastic manner. In this connection I am reminded of the prairie fire of enthusiasm that greeted the unpremeditated whimsey of two school girls recently in Bloomfield Hill, Michigan. Christina Darwell and Mary Jane Hiler, Kingswood High School seniors, were having lunch in the school cafeteria. On this particular day, bananas were being served. Each carried a small paper label. In a sudden freakish moment of odd-ball humor, both girls peeled off the labels and plastered them to the center of their foreheads.

Within a few moments kids at nearby tables wanted to know "what's the scoop?" In a twinkling of inspired imagination, the two girls informed their classmates, deadpan of course, that the fruit company would give a car to each person who saved up enough labels. "We plan," said Christina, "to get a sports car, and when it comes, we will raffle it off and give the money to the school scholarship fund."

For some unexplained reason, the story caught on with completely unexpected results. Classmates began collecting stickers. The school cafeteria staff took time out to peel stickers off every banana that came in. Before too long, faculty members, parents, and custodial workers were enlisted in the drive, and the girls suddenly found themselves literally knee-deep in stickers. When the faculty began wearing lapel badges reading "banana boosters," the girls panicked.

In desperation the pair carefully composed a letter to the fruit company in which they explained what had happened. "We have about ten thousand stickers on hand, and we don't know what to do with them. Do you have any suggestions?"

John M. Fox, president of United Fruit Company, himself an imaginative person, declared that such ingenuity should be properly rewarded. In a letter to the girls, he informed them that in return for 15,650 labels the company would endow a scholarship at Kingswood High School for $2,600.00 with the proviso that the beneficiary would be a student selected from one of the company schools in Central America. And so it was that a spontaneous spark took substance and opened up new vistas for ambitious youngsters in Latin America for years to come.

In Natural Law the Principle of Growth
Is Fundamental

In order to activate the first step that leads to increase, there are three elementary mental movements you must make. The fire-power that sets this immense energy to work is a tiny spark of wanting something. From this point on, the way opens up as if by magic.

1. Want something with a thirst that will not be denied.

2. Determine to take at least one step toward your goal every day.

3. Fire up your desire with strong interest and enthusiasm.

With these three fundamentals working for you, nothing can block your forward progress, for such is the force of the energies that were decreed for your use in the genesis of mankind. In fact, this is thinking like a millionaire with all the stops out.

Fortunately for the human race, there is no way to go in nature except forward. With this custom-built launching pad ready and waiting for your use, all you have to do is point your own finger of destiny. It is that simple. However, in this fundamental precept of growth there is an equally potent force that must be resisted. It is this: the opposite of growth is deterioration. Consequently, you have no choice. You either go forward to complete fulfillment, or you slip backward into mediocrity and merely vegetate. I know this is a terribly negative thought to inject into your consciousness at this time, but it is a fact of life which must be reckoned with.

There is no way to elude, or escape, the inevitability of natural law. Should all things seem to conspire against you, a simple prayer, asking for guidance, is one way to re-energize the forces of growth so that you will once again be moving toward a bright new future.

There Is No Limit to What You Can Accomplish

While I was in high school I knew a boy who had a burning desire to be a lawyer but family finances ruled out any possibility of his going to college. Even with this handicap, the lad was undaunted. First he landed a small clerking job in a local bank. His next step was to sign up for a course in commercial law in night school, where he wasn't satisfied with just the routine class assignments. He probed, asked questions of his superiors, and haunted the library for books related to the subject of his inspired interest.

Before too long this boy attracted the attention of the bank president. When a notary public was needed better to serve bank customers, he applied for and got the necessary credentials. This new responsibility caused him to learn all he could about his rights and obligations under the law. One day he happened to read the flamboyant ad of a homestudy course in law. With a small down payment, he subscribed for the service, knowing full well that a correspondence diploma would not be sufficient for him to be admitted to the bar.

However, in the pursuit of his studies, whole new avenues of legal practice were opened up to him and his quest for knowledge in the field of jurisprudence grew rapidly.

With this foundation he kept up to date by studying legal reports, attending seminars whenever he could, going to night classes, studying relevant law books so that he could follow the flow of legal papers through the bank, until eventually he felt that he had enough background to try for the bar examination.

It would be pleasing to say that he made it on his first attempt, but this was not destined to be true. However, he did manage to advance his knowledge of the law so much, as a result of this experience, that the following year, on his second try, he was able to pass with flying colors.

The First Step Is to Face Forward and Go, Go, Go!

No one, and I do mean no one, ever becomes a millionaire by his own efforts *unless he does two things:*

> 1. Makes up his or her mind that the comfortable status of wealth is precisely what is wanted.

> 2. Wants strongly enough to do something about it—no matter how small the gain—every day.

When I recall the careers of wealthy persons of my acquaintance, I am reminded of literally dozens of men and women who started with nothing and are now well off in terms of money, possessions, and achievement. Perhaps not all of them are millionaires, but at least they have gained a fair share of worldly abundance—enough to be financially independent and free from the enervating influence of want and privation.

The main thing is to start now, this very minute, with the declaration *I am going to be a millionaire.* Perhaps you won't make "big casino," but so what? You have, by this affirmation, lifted yourself out of the commonplace, and into the ranks of the well-to-do, for you have declared yourself a huge dividend that is yours, and yours alone. From this point on, all you have to do is to carefully tend the Law of Accrual, and it will take you just as far as you want to go.

Don't Stop to Count

As your gains begin to mount, one of the first restraints you have to learn is this: Don't pull the miserly stunt of stopping to count your increases, or your accomplishments. In the few minutes you take to "look back," you could master a new word, acquire a new fact, or practice a skill that is part of your growth pattern. You might just as well learn in the very beginning that gloating is for the birds. All it will ever gain for you is swelled ego, and surely you are smart enough to know that being self-centered has an effect exactly opposite to that of a gyroscope—instead of steadying a person on course, it tends to rock the boat of your forward progress, often quite violently.

One Thing Leads to Another

Once you have made the decision to steadily increase your assets of mind power and wealth, the next logical step is to expand your consciousness of money. This might sound like a crazy idea, but each and every one of us is as rich as we think, consequently it is quite essential that you learn how to open this door of awareness so that abundance in all things can flow into your life expression. In the next chapter you will discover how easy it is to take the next orderly step forward.

Summary

1. The natural Law of Accrual can be activated by any man, woman or child willing and able to take the first step forward.

2. Take a personal inventory of assets, such as educational background, experience values, and material possessions, and add the priceless ingredient of a positive daily performance of growth.

3. Since it is well known that a journey of a thousand miles begins with a single step, it just as naturally follows that the first movement is to possess some fact, or article, associated with the forward direction which you plan to travel.

4. When the course of direction is established, and the first measure of progress has been completed, the magic power of daily increase must be added to your steadily growing accumulation of skill, knowledge or wealth.

5. Always keep in mind that there is no way to escape the inevitability of natural law. A person either goes forward or he will succumb to mediocrity, or worse, go under. As of this moment, the free and easy choice is yours to make.

The Second Step to Riches

How to Develop a Money Consciousness

It has been established beyond the shadow of a doubt that each and every one of us is as rich as we think. It is a horse-sized pill to swallow, but it is the inescapable truth.

Money, just like water, seeks its own level; however, in this instance there is a startling variable. In a free economy each person draws his own money line and his pockets or his bank account promptly fills up to that level. The only catch to this delightful situation derives from one fact: unlike water, money flows slowly so it just might be a few weeks or even a few months before the steadily rising level of riches is noticeable. But *it will come to pass*—so powerful is the truth of natural law.

The problem confronting you now is: "How do I open up the floodgates so that the money I want will flow into my reservoir of available cash?"

The answer is so simple it is quite amazing why it escapes the attention of so many men and women. It is just like the story of Acres of Diamonds, or the lesser-known account of the man who left his rocky hillside home in Colorado to journey west with the gold-seeking hordes of forty-niners. Years later, broke and disheartened, he returned home to find that he had been living on top of one of the richest mineral deposits ever discovered in the west.

That is precisely what you are doing at this very minute. All you have to do is raise your level of consciousness. In a practical sense, this means raise your money consciousness. In truth, you don't have to be a millionaire—just *think* like one—not in the stupid illusions of gambling, or other doltish get-rich-quick schemes, but in the bright consciousness of right money, rightly acquired.

How to Use the "Attitude of Expectancy"

Begin today to affirm with great feeling and intensity, "I now have all the money I want. I have plenty of money in my pockets, in my bank account, or available for my use." Repeat, repeat, and repeat this declaration with great purpose until the magic of believing takes over and you have turned the flow of money, or credit, into your waiting coffers. It is this attitude of unrelenting expectancy that will eventually bring you great riches.

It is indeed unfortunate that banks, insurance companies, savings and loan associations, and, worst of all, school banking programs put far too much emphasis on saving for a rainy day and none whatever on the powerfully motivating force of a money consciousness. Without any question the idea of thrift is a wonderful trait of character to nurture along as it pertains to growth, but certainly not as a means of attaining great wealth.

I will grant quite willingly that thrift and habits of frugal living will create small fortunes, and occasionally time and circumstances will serve to build vast holdings of money and property, but the grim truth of the matter is that a thousand times more abundance of mind and affluence sprouts from a money consciousness than from all of the savings plans ever devised.

Quite obviously the foregoing is contrary to the accepted behavior patterns of today, but who in blazes wants to be a conformist? Be rich in mind, spirit and money, for it is only with these attributes of character and possessions that you will be enabled to live your particular life expression abundantly.

Since the "proof of the pudding usually dribbles all over the shirt front" you can rightfully ask, "What has this bright idea ever done for you?" Well, the uncompromising truth is that I was reared in a Scottish family where every tradition of thrift and frugality was regarded as a way of life. Frankly, it took me more than half a century to escape the bonds of my stern and inflexible upbringing, but a chance observation by our minister let in a faint ray of light, and my search for unfoldment was on in full force with the results little short of fantastic.

How You Can Develop a Money Consciousness

Now you will want to know, "What can I do to develop a money consciousness?" Each individual starts with a different level of money awareness; consequently, the problem will vary with each person. To put the situation even more bluntly, there is no glib, general statement that will apply in each and every particular to all men. However, there is a bright beam of light emanating from five extremely cogent directives. These are:

1. Develop an insatiable curiosity.

2. Grow a little in wealth and mind power every day.

3. Constantly affirm with great feeling the declaration presented in the first part of this guideline to riches, "I now have all the money I want. . . ."

4. Read significant books in or near the area of your occupation.

5. Gradually acquire a bank account of contacts.

Since all of these suggestions will be fully explored in forthcoming chapters, suffice it to say here that this business of developing an insatiable curiosity will be examined next in a manner that will be startling if not provocative, and moreover, the ideas in action can open up a whole new way of life for you.

How to Zero In on One Target

The second vitally important step to thinking in terms of abundance has so many well-marked pathways that it took months of painstaking research to find the most practical and useful route to follow. To begin with, solid and dependable vision is founded on a selective curiosity. This urge to gain information unfortunately has a negative, as well as an affirmative, direction. One leads to fantastic success while the other ends up 'way off in the boondocks of pure nosiness and frustration, because little of value can be learned from minding somebody else's business.

How to Use the Ten-Point Plan of Increase

Since we are only concerned here with the positive aspects of our program of growth, the ten-point plan of steadily expanding increase is presented for your use.

With a practical and well-ordered curiosity focused upon one endeavor, there is no place else to go except forward with ever-increasing speed. The special stratagem, if there is one, is to direct one's attention to a single intense interest, a single strong intent, one attainable goal at a time.

A Scrapbook Is Helpful

Most persons with an all-consuming interest in one subject or activity keep a scrapbook or at least one file in which any related data can be pasted or saved for future reference. This practice is the cornerstone of increase in any activity, but the first step in building an awareness of money is to impart an hydraulic lift to the level of consciousness. This habit of daily growth automatically raises a uniform and well balanced expansion of the mental horizons that you are seeking.

When we have established beyond any reservation the topic, trade, profession, or objective that we are going to pursue, and get going in the direction of an ever-expanding money consciousness, the next movement is to include a program of balance in our plan of action.

A Realistic Ten Point Plan That Insures Growth

1. The first act, guaranteed to raise the level of consciousness that includes money awareness, is a concentrated and enthusiastic regard for one practical area of endeavor regardless of what it is.

2. Begin to collect all of the available information in or near your subject of interest, and fit what you have learned into an organized pattern of growth.

3. Accept the fact that in order to increase your holdings or advantages you have to think big in order to grow big—all the time knowing full well that you have to keep "one foot on the ground."

4. Repeat, repeat, repeat the suggestion in the first step: "I now have all the money I need in my pockets, in my bank account, or available for my future plans." You might view this suggestion as completely wacky, especially in the beginning, but I dare you to try it for one year.

5. Never, never, never and I mean *never* permit yourself the expensive luxury of thinking or saying, "I can't afford it." It is far more positive and uplifting to say, "When the right time comes along I will have this thing I want." With this strong affirmative declaration constantly emphasized, your money consciousness will grow as if you had been touched by a miracle.

6. Learn to regard money as a commodity of numbered pieces of metal and paper—as a means to an end—and not the end itself designed to serve your purpose.

7. Never be satisfied with the steps you have taken. The reason for this is plain. The day you stop taking that forward step your growth toward the high plateau of accomplishment is retarded. Remember always that even as little as one penny a day saved or one new fact absorbed will one day bring you unlimited rewards.

8. Now that we have established a base for the proper cultivation of a money consciousness, it is time to acquaint you with measures of balance designed to impart strength and clarity of perception to all of your objectives. These special attributes come under the broad term of background. This essential backdrop of personality is the wide-angle screen against which all of your traits of character, unusual advantages, skills, talents, and your storehouse of specialized knowledge is played in order for your contemporaries to evaluate you as an effective individual.

9. Included in the ninth point of our program of development there are nine sub-titles that will serve to help you build background. All of these primary blast-off pads cannot be put into action in a single day, but all of them can be activated at appropriate times and preferably employed as a breather in your steadily growing plan of development:

a. Travel

b. Attend plays of literary stature
c. Take an evening off to enjoy an opera or symphony
d. Learn to fluently read and write a foreign language
e. Read a good novel or a worthwhile nonfiction book
f. Attend a variety of sporting events
g. Socialize discreetly and with a purpose
h. Take an active, but restrained, part in community affairs
i. Attend lectures of quality where matters of some substance are discussed

The foregoing list will provide a launching platform from which any career can be boosted into the upper strata of money awareness. However, note the addition of cultural values at the end of the program and not as a prelude to a systematic plan of increase.

10. Build a genuine interest in these values:
a. Have an appropriate concern for government and civic enterprise
b. Set up a far-reaching program covering the topics of business and/or industry
c. Learn all you can about banking and matters of finance at all levels
d. Make it a point to be informed about educational facilities or research projects in or near your occupation
e. Seek out and take advantage of every opportunity to visit the plants of any one of these activities and try, whenever possible, for a brief interview with the head man *if* you have a sensible question to ask

The Fable of the Little Acorn

Most persons are familiar with the ancient proverb, "Big oaks from little acorns grow," but the fact which isn't included in this aphorism is that this solid growth often covers a span of several generations. When the full circumstances of increase are evaluated in perspective one can quickly understand why it is recommended that you save as little as one penny a day.

It really boils down to this: The basic idea is to establish an over-all pattern of growth. And it isn't the amount of capital that is saved or employed, it is the power of the additive of imagination that you inject into the enterprise of your choosing. Fortunately this special ingredient is free—ready and waiting for your use this minute.

By this time nearly everyone in the country has heard of Colonel Sanders and his recipe for preparing Kentucky fried chicken. The lightning of creativity failed to strike this genial person until he had reached the full retirement age of sixty-five, but with his first Social Security check of $104 he managed to build an empire of franchised chicken stands all over the country. He retired again, ten years later, with an estate of several million dollars.

How to Use the Explosive Power of the Unearned Increment

When any man or woman thinks like a millionaire he or she uses an old economics precept or formula, hoping for a sudden irresistible increase. The basic theory is this: An idea, plus imagination, plus an X number of dollars, equals a fantastic success—providing, of course, that your plans are applied ahead of a forward moving trend of human needs. Fundamentally this rule of thumb has some drawbacks because of the unknowns—the other x's and y's that serve to mess up the best laid projects. This happens because most persons are not fully informed about all of the side effects of contention that must be faced.

It is for this purpose that the several rudiments of fast growth are spelled out for your immediate use in the fifteen steps Not one of the parts can be evaded or skipped over.

It is essential that every one of them be worked into an integrated plan or the whole system will come unglued.

How to Use Three More Strong Money Consciousness Boosters

There are many ways to raise the level of consciousness, some of which have already been presented for your use. There are three additional solid fuel boosters that possess immense power building potentials which are not always so favorably considered. The reason for this stand-offish attitude probably derives from the fact that the art of learning is too often identified with the sometimes tedious programs imposed upon luckless students by dull or unimaginative school administrators.

This situation is indeed unfortunate. The incontrovertible fact is that learning is a lifetime enterprise. It is dismaying to witness the actual mental deterioration of good students, some college graduates, even a few with advanced degrees in various areas of accomplishment, all because the level of consciousness was allowed to shrivel away for lack of a challenging mental nutrition program.

The degree of knowing either grows or is retarded by the diet of information that is fed into it, but the startling fact that is difficult for most persons to comprehend is that a money consciousness is a special trait of character that only *you* can make active and meaningful.

In order to avoid a lessening of our natural heritage of ability to grow, to expand, and to increase our holdings—both mental and material—it is quite important for us to know that in our complex of development these three basic objectives should loom very large:

1. The ability to speak intelligently to any group of persons. This can easily be achieved by any man or woman by joining

your nearest Toastmaster or Toastmistress Club—not for the purpose of becoming a silver-tongued orator, but for the sole intent of broadening one's viewpoint by adjusting, in a friendly and cooperative fashion, to the thinking of other persons. This is one of the few forms of positive friction that I know of with a strong tendency to build mind power.

2. Maintain an aggressive interest in a practical hobby. This can be any activity that will put high voltage into the priceless ingredient of interest. The hobby selected should have practical overtones because it leads so easily into the third and final booster program.

3. A study project. This can be immensely valuable, especially when it is tied in with actually handling the tools, implements, materials, vegetation, animals, or minerals of your extra-curricular activity.

Why Possessions Won't Bring Happiness, But Happiness Will Bring Possessions

Without any question happiness is an exalted level of consciousness, but there is a joker in the deck. The whole tenuous fabric must be held together with strong affirmations of good—not only for yourself, but for all of the persons with whom you associate.

What has happiness to do with an awareness of money? The answer is really quite simple. Without the full spark of joy that goes into the daily living process, it is easy to pull the plug on the whole enterprise that is you, and a patiently built-up level of consciousness can drain away in a matter of hours unless sturdy fingers are pushed into the dyke. These can be declarations of expected increase that will not be denied and are sustained by an attitude of expectancy that will be fully explained for your use in the fourth step. This hazard is mentioned because the ingredients that go into the creation of a vibrant level of consciousness are both fragile and often volatile, especially during the formative years.

It is true that the things you come to own won't always be tangible, but one thing is for sure, the things you come to possess won't be worth a tinker's damn unless you can accept them gladly, knowing full well that what you have on hand is only on loan from the power that granted you the right to use them.

Money, Money, Money

As a beginning researcher into the vast powers of the mind, I met briefly a young woman—casualty of an early marriage, left alone with nothing but the clothes on her back and a cash capital of sixty dollars. In recounting her experiences she informed me on more than one occasion that she made the word, "money" her watchword, so determined was she never again to be broke. She repeated the word "money" so often that it became part of her consciousness. This was done without her losing her sense of balance.

While this strong affirmation of the word "money" soon attracted a steadily growing flow of funds into her hands, it was not long before she discovered that there were other equally energized forces that helped to magnetize her purpose. More in jest than anything else at the time I suggested some of the methods that I am now advancing for your use—but this gal was so hungry for ways and means that she took my ideas seriously; so much so in fact that she is now not only tops in her career, but she is also independently wealthy.

In another instance there was a young man broken in

health and spirit and almost fresh out of capital who regarded a small piece of dry sea vegetation in a far away
Japanese fishing village with great interest. He'd heard
tales in Tokyo about the longevity of the men and women
who inhabited this isolated spot. When the facts were made
known to him, he declared, "This product will one day
make me a million dollars." And it was this strong and
highly energized affirmation that founded the giant multi-
million-dollar Organic Sea Food Corporation of San Francisco, now nearly fifty years in successful operation.

You Can Start Your Increase Today

The beginning of any great fortune is founded upon a
money consciousness. And this awareness can be raised to
any level you want right this very moment. All you have
to do to start this irresistible lifting force working for you
is to declare with intensity, "I now plant the seed of great
wealth in my consciousness," and begin this very day to
create your foundation, using the easy building blocks provided for your use.

Now that you have raised the level of your consciousness to include an abundant supply of money, the next essential step is to get fully in stride with the rhythm of the
success cycle. This cadence—that is, being in step with good
fortune—is a force that must be reckoned with if you would
go forward to your greatest potential. In order to achieve
the most benefit from this part of natural law, you must
learn to recognize this ebb-and-flow of advantage so that
you can go into high gear when the rhythm of attraction is
on in full force.

All of the positive techniques you will need to know
will be fully outlined for your use in the next growth step.

Summary

1. It is now established as a basic truth that every man, woman and child marks his own level of money or success consciousness.

2. This point of awareness of money or accomplishment can be pegged on the highest mountain of achievement if you but will it that way.

3. To begin your climb to riches, all you have to do is declare with great emphasis, "I now have all the money I want in my pocket, in the bank, or available for my use," and go on to make this powerful declaration come true without once looking back.

4. You can create a foundation of immense tensile strength simply by activating the ten consciousness boosters and then support their upward thrust with the three second-stage propellents.

5. You can start the beginnings of great wealth this very instant, but it is you and you alone who can plant the seed and provide the growing material.

How to Engage the Success
Cycle

Oddly enough, even the seemingly elusive quality of success has an ebb-and-flow rhythm. Just as "The Music Goes 'Round and 'Round"—or the rotor on an electric light meter twirls when in use, so does the transient wand of success touch each and every one of us at varying intervals of time.

When Lincoln first ventured into his professional career he declared, "I will prepare and some day my chance will come." Shakespeare phrased the same idea in the soliloquy of Brutus in *Julius Caesar:*

*There is a tide in the affairs of men,
Which, taken at the flood, leads on to fortune;
Omitted, all the voyage of their life
Is bound in shallows and in miseries.*

Therefore, one of the first requisites in learning to think like a millionaire is to make a firm and very determined resolution to be an outstanding expert in *something*—but whatever old or new and untried activity you center upon, resolve with great will to learn and assimilate all there is to know about the subject you have chosen.

This single, intensely directed interest in any given field of endeavor has never yet failed to produce a boundless richness of mind as well as enormous holdings of wealth plus an achievement record well noted by one's contemporaries.

How to Use Selective Curiosity

Two words that adequately describe the millionaire potential are *selective curiosity*.

It is important to differentiate between the ordinary trait of nosiness and the powerful highly-energized characteristic of a strongly-motivated quest for knowledge within a specialized area of endeavor. This tendency to probe, to study and compare, to research, and to inquire into every phase of given activity, is the one essential quality that separates the men from the dreamers in the quest for success, achievement, and great wealth.

This urge to know, as expressed in the careers of successful men and women, embraces every imaginable field of activity including salesmanship, business, the trades, and even the professions that demand a long and tedious period of preparation. I like to tell the story of a janitor in a great Eastern school of medicine who once nurtured an insatiable thirst for learning all there was to know about healing the sick. In seeking his ultimate fulfillment, this man began to collect from every classroom in the building assigned to him for clearing textbooks that had been discarded by the students. At night, in his lonely basement room in the dormitory this chap would read and study endlessly—until one day he was publicly recognized by this same university as one of the outstanding diagnosticians of his time—even though he did not hold a formal degree in medicine.

In another instance, I once knew a young fellow who became obsessed with a burning desire to own his own print shop. To begin with, this man knew from nothing about the trade, but he did possess one priceless ingredient of character—selective curiosity. Out of his meagre earnings as a day laborer on the shipping docks of a trucking company, he began to read everything he could get his hands on pertaining to the trade. By literally saving his pennies he was one day able to acquire a small handpress, a few sticks of furniture to help compress and hold type within a given space, and one font of old type. With an apparently dismal start, this man began to attract other items associated with the craft until one day he was able to take the big plunge and open a modest little shop of his own. Today this determined individual is the full owner of a large and flourishing printing business.

There are innumerable "little success stories" just like these to be found in nearly every walk of life. *The same can be done by you*—but you are the only person in the world who can set this success cycle with its magic wand moving toward you and your enterprises.

Make These Five Moves and You Are "On the Bandwagon"

1. Determine to increase your wealth potential each and every day even if all you do is add one penny to your capital account. When you perform this act of adding to, know that it is for the purpose of establishing a pattern of daily growth.

2. Determine to raise your level of money consciousness to the height of one million dollars—and learn to keep your attitudes oriented to this high plateau of achievement.

3. Direct your attention to the broad field of human interests and determine precisely what it is that you are going to grow with—be it animal, food, flowers, a service, a trade, a pro-

fession, or a device. Regardless of what it is, what you choose is to be your through, one-way ticket to whatever it is that you want to accomplish.

4. Determine to follow the growth patterns as described in each of the fifteen steps to thinking like a millionaire, in the exact order as they are given herein.

5. Develop your own time plan of growth. In brief, this means to set forth in your own blueprint for personal progress, the list of accomplishments that you must acquire in order to reach your goal—with the full understanding that a great success is founded upon the law of minor achievement. In practice this means that the summit of complete fulfillment can only be attained by adding together hundreds of little successes.

Once you are on the bandwagon of increase there can be no limit to how far you can go. You set the goal and the wagon begins to move irresistibly.

One Man Started With a Handful
of Montana Wheat

Back at the turn of the century, Thomas Donald Campbell, a small cattle rancher, regarded a handful of scrawny plains wheat. What he saw did not please him, so he determined to do something about it. He set himself the task of applying modern methods of agriculture to the growing of better wheat, with a greater yield per acre. Before too long he was confronted with the necessity of applying the newly invented techniques of mechanization to his farm operations. The lists of his attainments are legion, and the results of his keen interest in a few grains of wheat have made history.

When Campbell passed away recently he was farming 95,000 acres of land in Montana and directing the operation of a land holding in New Mexico that totaled close to a half-million acres. For these achievements he was widely regarded as "America's Wheat King." All because he directed a strong selective curiosity toward the prime ingredient of a loaf of bread—a human need that has pre vailed since the beginning of time.

In between there were endless minor achievements, but the pinnacle of his growth was attained when more than a dozen foreign governments recognized his genius, including such nations as Russia, Britain, and France, and engaged him to assist in the development of millions of acres of farm land in which the principles of soil management, crop rotation, and mechanization were put into practice.

How to Get Aboard the Success Cycle

Probably the first thought that occurs to you will be: "This is going to take some doing." In truth, however, the ticket that is needed to get into the full rhythm of success is so close, and so obvious, that all too many persons look right past a dozen opportunities to grow rich each and every day. Again, all that you need to do is direct your undivided attention toward any item that sparks your interest and then apply the three-point system of evaluation explained in the next few paragraphs.

Getting the right answer might demand a bit of study, but the rewards are so immense that the trifle of effort required is of little consequence.

The Three-Point System of Evaluation

1. Is the item you have selected practical? In other words, is it even with or just a little ahead of present trends in human

interest? To select an idea, a product, service, or a device that is too far in advance of acceptance is to load yourself down with an impossible burden of sales and distribution problems and you will further handicap yourself because of the need for heavy advertising expenditures. Make certain that what you have in mind is almost ready to ride the crest of popular demand. How to do this most effectively is fully explained in the Fifth Step.

2. Is the item you have selected in or near a basic human want? Perhaps the buying public doesn't know what it wants, much less needs, your product or idea, but testing can often reveal the answer. Employ all of the techniques explained in Step Five when you are far enough along to make this part of your working equipment.

3. What is the growth or profit potential of the product, device, service, or idea that sparks your interest? And there is still another question that should back up this first query: Is this idea of yours likely to hit now, or will it take years of hard work?

The essential challenge is this: "Is what I have in mind better, bigger, faster, lovelier? Does it provide a chance for greater returns, or insure an easier way of life?"

Why is this careful review necessary? For example, in the food and grocery business alone last year more than 2500 new products were introduced to the buying public, and out of this number more than a thousand items were discarded for the very plain reason that the housewife didn't cotton to the idea. Unfortunately, most of these discards came from firms or persons who dived headlong into the production of a product simply because it appealed to them. In other words then, when you are truly thinking like a millionaire you will first learn to evaluate correctly.

You might be justified in claiming that anything you choose will get you into the full rhythm of the success cycle, but let's take a closer look.

Grab a Brass Ring

When I first proclaimed the theory of "anything goes" in a talk to the Beverly Hills Kiwanis Club, I could literally see the eyebrows of successful business and professional men in the audience climb up their foreheads, but two men in attendance that day didn't laugh. One was a manager of a small employment agency and the other was a self-styled poet. Today the first man is head of a nation-wide employment service with branches in many cities and his daily income is still climbing in a most fantastic manner. The second man spoke to me after the meeting and among other things he said, "I want to be Poet Laureate of California. Do you think I can make it?" My reply: "If you have what it takes, yes." This man looked me squarely in the eye and replied, "I believe I have."

Five years later, almost to the day, this determined person sent me a telegram from the State Capitol in Sacramento, saying, "Unanimous approval rules committee. Waiting in Assembly for final passage." And so it was that on June 10, 1953, Gordon W. Norris was made the fourth Poet Laureate of California in a joint session of the legislature—simply because he believed in himself so strongly that he never quit trying.

On another occasion I was having lunch with an aspiring motion picture star in the commissary at Universal Studios in Hollywood. The girl was young and lovely with an accent that was heavily West Indian and possessed of a driving ambition. She knew that to reach stardom in a town that overflowed with beautiful women, something more than just beauty was necessary. She had it—an unusual idea. She said to me, "I believe people of all ages will like fairy tales. I want to do something like Arabian Nights."

At the time I treated the idea lightly, but in less than two years I had to eat crow. When the picture *Arabian Nights* was shown to the press, Maria Montez couldn't resist winking impishly at me as she walked from the studio preview theatre. From that moment on, whenever a wild idea was broached to me, I wisely kept my comments to myself.

A Bonanza From "Dogs"

'Way back in 1919 an enterprising haberdasher by the name of Walter Nordlinger startled the merchandising world half out of its stolid wits. The town was Washington, D. C. and the time was shortly after the close of World War I, when business could have been better. In this situation, Nordlinger had a problem. Too much window exposure had faded some of his stock of expensive shirts. At the asking price no one was interested, so this man put a quick sale tag of 50¢ on them and on that day custom was born.

Since that inauspicious beginning, customers from miles around Washington look forward to the huge Washington's Birthday sales, because now everybody gets into the act. All that is needed to unload huge quantities of odds and ends of left-over items is to put a price on them. At first the Better Business Bureau took a dim view of the situation, but time and success soon softened this opposition although they admit that some merchants take advantage of the buying spirit of enthusiastic customers to palm off shoddy goods.

Be that as it may, there are few complaints. Most persons know that they get what they pay for—and the chesterfield coat that sold for less than ten dollars still comes close to looking like its original value of $125.00.

Even a Rose Can Make You Rich

Not too many persons know that if you can create a new type of rose the United States Patent Office will protect your horticultural product with an exclusive grant to market for a period of seventeen years. And that isn't all. Should you christen your rose by an unusual or exotic name, or name it after a famous personality, the title you have selected for your creation can be registered and thus protect your idea permanently.

During the years the list of rose names included in the International Rose Register has climbed steadily until now the total is nearing the ten thousand mark. Quite an achievement for a mere flower.

Anything Goes

The reason I cite these several commonplace ideas is for the sole purpose of making it clear that anything goes. There isn't a single everyday item that you can name that doesn't contain the elements of great fortune. All you have to do is think beyond the obvious. You can start your prospecting venture by asking yourself a few simple questions about the idea, product or device that you are contemplating, such as:

1. Will an interest-compelling name help?

2. Is there a new or different use for this item lurking here unseen?

3. Could this idea be adapted and used in some other field?

In my talks to service clubs and civic groups covering my favorite topic of innovation I like to emphasize these points. Naturally enough, this is a challenge that is frequently accepted by persons in the audience. Often the product or service of a questioner will be mentioned. On more than one occasion this completely inadequate, off-the-cuff brainstorming will cause more than one person to comment, "Well, what do you know about this!"

At other times someone present will hand me an ordinary product and ask, "What can you do with this?" During one question-and-answer period, one of the men present handed me a tenpenny nail. This item is about as low in the scale of commonplace things as you can go since it was one of the very early inventions of man, but a sudden inspiration hit me. "What," I asked, "would you think of a nail that would do so-and-so?"

"Mister," this chap retorted, "if you can do that, our firm alone will make you a millionaire." As I am writing this, I can't tell you how it is going to turn out, but I am presently directing all twelve of my precious mind powers to solving the problem. And I have the strongest feeling it can be done.

How to Spot a "Sleeper"

The man or woman who is always thinking like a millionaire does three things as a matter of habit:

1. He looks beyond the obvious, even in ordinary things.

2. He learns to estimate the value of any item over and above its commonplace appearance or usage.

3. He learns to raise his sights. That is, he looks over all the routine outlets for the item, and then lets his money consciousness take a broad, high look for new, and perhaps completely different sources of interest.

"Getting a Corner" On Old Street Corner Signs

Does that heading sound goofy? Wait until you have read the story. It seems that one Libby O'Brien accomplished this very thing. It all happened in such a prosy manner that the good lady almost passed up a tidy fortune.

One day Miss O'Brien was traveling to her home in Old Greenwich, Connecticut, when she happened to glance out of the window of the New Haven train and saw a huge pile of old street signs piled up in a vacant lot in the Bronx. For almost half a-century New York had marked its street intersections with big iron signs, painted blue, with white lettering. Late in the fall of the previous year, the city began to replace the ancient markers with smaller yellow signs with black letters, and the old signs had to be dumped. Here they were in a vacant lot. The pile grew and grew until the unsightly heap caught the attention of a fast-thinking woman.

Early the next morning, Libby O'Brien went searching. Before too long she was directed to the city's department of traffic. To her inquiry, "Are the signs for sale?" she got a terse retort, "Why not? Make us a bid." And this she did. Right out of her head she picked the figure of $478.00— probably because that was the amount she had tucked away in her cookie jar. At any rate her bid was accepted, especially since no one else seemed to be interested. With the signs now her legal property, she was faced with a moving and marketing problem in that order. The city had given her thirty days to remove the "junk."

The little lady tackled her problem with imagination. She began parading her wares through Grand Central Sta tion, with gratifying results. Her pile of 10,000 old signs began to disappear rapidly at prices ranging from ten to fifty dollars. Not bad for a quick look out of a train window.

And Then There Is "Space"

With all of a thousand pieces of hardware floating around "up there" some hard-thinking person is going to come up with a salvaging idea one of these days and become a millionaire overnight. Especially since more junk is going into orbit each week. And recovery of these floating monstrosities isn't the only source of wealth from the space program. Imaginative firms all over the nation are now working on kits, tools, and devices that will serve to make the "moon project" more rewarding, or other delves into outer space more revealing.

You Can "Think and Grow Rich," But First You Have to Put On Your "Million Dollar Glasses"

Once as I traveled into Hollywood from my home in Riverside, I donned my rose-colored glasses just for fun. The trip is only about sixty miles, but in that brief passage I counted nine potential money-making opportunities that were apparently going begging for lack of a taker. This lamentable situation could only derive from one thing. The men and women driving into town were too concerned with the problems of the day, such as home, business, or who said what to whom, instead of looking for chances to make money that seem to be everywhere. I am quite positive that if the situation I have described prevails in Southern California, a comparatively new settlement, there are 10,000 more opportunities in older sections of the country

—like the street signs rusting away on a vacant lot in the Bronx.

There Is a Money-Making Reason

For every idea, device, or product that is created, there is always the potential of thousand variations. It is up to you to examine with imagination commonplace products or services.

Every time you open the door on anything new or different or expand the utility of an ordinary item, you are opening up vistas of accomplishment that can extend down the brightly lit "corridors of time." On the face of it this might appear just a little too poetic, but the truth of the matter is plain. Like space, there is no limit to the future.

There is only one word of caution. Within the context of the guideline you are now reading, it is quite essential that you build your road to great riches one block at a time and the next step you are going to take is the cement that will bind your own avenue to wealth together as solidly as the Appian Way that held the vast Roman Empire as one.

Summary

1. The first move any individual must make in order to get in the white water flow of the success cycle is to become an outstanding expert in something.

2. The next move is to grab a brass ring—that is, pick an idea, an item, a product, or a service, either lay or professional, and find something in that single thing to seize on to mentally—because what you select for special interest is a freeway ticket to great accomplishment, regardless of what sparks your attention

3. Should you need guidance in determining what to concentrate on, begin to sort, choose and eliminate until you have sharpened the natural tool of selective curiosity to a razor-thin edge, and then you will be able to pick that which is good for you.

4. When you find what you want, direct your attention to the *five moves* that will provide you with a permanent place on the crest of the success cycle and ride it out.

5. And remember always, even the most commonplace of ideas, events, or products contain the seeds of great fortune. All you have to do is to wear your rose-colored glasses and look beyond the obvious.

What the Attitude of Expectancy
Will Do for You

This precept may appear to be unimportant. In fact most persons confronted with this simple directive tend to brush it off as so much hokum or sentimental matter introduced for the purpose of effect, but when the real truth is known and understood, a whole new way of life can be revealed to an enlightened man or woman within a matter of hours.

To begin with, a true attitude of expectancy cannot be properly implemented until certain forthright and positive acts of will are given the force of dynamic mind power. Should this sound a little bit heavy I have some disturbing news for you—you haven't heard the half of it yet.

In order to be thinking like a really successful millionaire, a certain mental house-cleaning must be achieved. To do this job effectively, the conscious mind must be cleansed of all that is unworthy: This includes all

1. Hates, be they petty or great

2. Fears, be they founded in fact or imagination

3. Resentments, be they founded in petty slights or very real grievances, and

4. Superstitions, be they founded in fun or fearsome relics of the dark ages.

In other words, release the past from your consciousness, regardless of the sources of your displeasure or the depth of your dislikes.

This is a king-sized order, but it can be accomplished within a matter of minutes if you sincerely want to think like and be a millionaire. All that is required is a simple act of powerfully-motivated will power.

Once this cleansing process has been energized by a determined and strongly declared affirmation it must be sustained. In order to give meaning and direction to this newly-acquired way of life, every assault made upon your conscious mind by the four snares must be met with a vigorous and overwhelming counter-attack. In other words, once the mind is cleansed of rubbish, keep it free of the filth that eats away at your power to attain a richness of mind, and your ability to acquire and hold great wealth.

How to Be Prepared For Riches

It is true that in the beginning it will take some real doing to keep the mind free and clear of these undermining thoughts. But there is one delightfully bright and inspiring result that is soon in evidence: with each repulse of these down-beat influences, the attacks of negativeness will begin to wane until finally the mind is able to develop a true and completely valid attitude of expectancy. When this is accomplished, you can then truly assert with great emphasis:

1. I am grateful for all of the good that has come to me this day.

2. I know that I am going to win because what I want is right for me, my customers, or my associates.

3. I know that I am now being enriched in body, mind and spirit and my store of wealth is being increased this day because I am now prepared to accept my good fortune.

When you have really activated all of the suggestions that are offered for your use in this important step, you will have truly acquired an attitude of expectancy that will not be denied any accomplishment. The whole meaning and import of your life will begin to take on a new highly-energized vitality when "all things will be added unto you."

How long this will take is hard to say. Some persons have witnessed the miracle of change within one day, while it took other persons a week or even a month. The reason it is difficult to give you an accurate answer stems from one fact: No one knows how deeply imbedded in your mind are the self-inflicted distractions of the past. However, once you get a glimpse of the truth about yourself you should never falter for one second longer than it takes to organize a counter attack of powerful affirmations. The results will speak for themselves.

When Your Thoughts Turn Into "Things"

Now that you have learned the easy steps to strong affirmative thinking, you can only wonder at the abysmal negativeness that seems to prevail. In fact, you will feel so elated over your new-found awareness that you would like to shout it from the housetops, but you should be fully conscious of the skepticism that would greet such an antic.

To begin with, this positive attitude—this anticipation of achieving greatly—can be given an energized push forward every time you increase your capital by as little as one cent, or add to your store of working knowledge by one dynamic thought. The trick of growing here must be sustained by an unrelenting attitude of confident growth.

The attitude of expectancy can only expand and mature in a mental soil that accepts no thought but increase, regardless of any untoward circumstance that might develop. Perhaps it will take some doing to create this pose, especially in the beginning when the mental climate still has an overhang of the blues. But it can be accomplished and with comparatively little effort, simply by having a power-packed affirmation ready to counter-attack any tendency to give in to the intrusion of a down-beat idea. In this way your thoughts can turn your way of life into all the things that build growth and increase.

How to Do a "Right-About-Face"

This command is familiar to all persons who have suffered through tedious hours of close order drill, but in the field of mind power it possesses a connotation that can't be ignored. Walt Newman, a moderately successful salesman, got this message one day when he lost a fairly good-sized order simply because he wasn't fully prepared for contention with a customer; and worse, he had to admit to himself that he didn't expect to get a valid signature on the old dotted line anyway. As he walked out of the man's place of business, he demanded of himself, "What in blazes is the matter with me anyway?" Since he was alone, the question was purely rhetorical; but in that moment of self-evaluation Walt determined to find out.

Later in the day and quite by accident while Walt was waiting to keep an appointment with a customer, he picked up a copy of *Millionaire* magazine that contained a small part of the material you are now reading. When he had finished studying the piece he couldn't help but declare

out loud, "So that's what's the matter with me!" To say that
the queen of the reception desk was startled would be putting it mildly.

In any event Walt made up his mind right then and there
to right-about-face. He would think only positive thoughts.
He would always expect to win. And he would never, never
make a call again when he wasn't fully prepared to talk to
the customer in terms of profit and advantage. From that
moment on his sales began to climb. So much so, in fact,
that before too long he was the fair-haired boy of the sales
department—and a year later when the salesmanager was
promoted to a branch office assignment in the East, Walt
stepped into his job.

When You Know How—It Is Easy

There are nine ways to counter-attack any invasion of
ideas that are contrary to the attitude of expectancy. And
the basic cause in all of these directives grows out of one
single, easily acquired state of mind. Always expect to win.
There can be no deviation from this success stance, regardless of the turn of events. The trick is to find some good in
everything that happens, and keep right on going. It is
precisely as one wise philosopher put it, "It isn't how hard
you fall, it's how high you bounce that counts."

Now let's get on with the job of making the nine points
of progress part of your daily growth pattern.

Positive Preparedness. This particular mental pose has two
parts. One is always to be prepared with a positive program
of action, and the other is to have ready a powerful affirmative declaration whenever the slightest taint of discourage-
ment creeps into consciousness. Like a dark cloud these
attitudes can sneak in on us when we are not looking

mentally. Yet unless they are blown out instantly, they can quickly overwhelm our thoughts with so many ideas of defeat that we lose all perspective.

There are many ways to forestall this hazard of downbeat thinking, but the one that I like to tell about came from a delightful personality in her late eighties. It seems this charming little lady was harassed with the usual platitudes of gloom like, "It is the Lord's will," "No matter how hard I try everything seems to go wrong," "I never win anything," "That's the way the ball always bounces," and so on ad nauseam.

One day this person, let's call her Clara, found that whenever she thought of flowers she just seemed to light up inside like a Christmas tree. Before too long she discovered that whenever the inevitable thoughts of disaster began to intrude, all she had to do was think of her lovely flowers and whammo, the blues disappeared as if by magic.

In the beginning, Clara relates, she was thinking about flowers most of the time, but as she grew in her new awareness, she was able to get out of her mental flower garden and reach a new level of consciousness. From this point on her progress was fantastic. Her health improved almost overnight. Her family finances were soon in good order, and she had time that she had never seemed to have before for church and club activities.

Perhaps flowers aren't your particular cup of tea, but somewhere in your consciousness there is a key that will release for you the positive power of always expecting good things to happen to you—and they will. Not always perhaps, but you will be better able to cope with adverse happenings, and thus be back in the race and running again without too much loss of valuable time.

Anticipation. Learning how to always anticipate all of the good that can come to you is one thing, but knowing how to *rev* up this feeling to its maximum pitch is something else. The reason why this highly energized emotion is so essential to the millionaire level of awareness is this: An attitude of expectancy creates new and powerful forces of alertness, vigilance, astuteness—and eventually, foresight. It is just as I heard the brilliant editorial writer Arthur Brisbane once tell a complaining writer, "If you don't expect to win—you won't."

However, there is a catch to this seemingly ingenuous phrase. Anticipation takes you up to the door all bright-eyed and bushy-tailed, but once the door is open, it is absolutely essential that you have another highly desirable goal ready and waiting to pursue with ever more expectation, else you are not truly thinking like a millionaire. This truth demonstrates precisely why a blueprint for growth and progress is so necessary, spelled out in terms of increase for tomorrow, next week, next year, and so on until your ultimate goal of achievement is fulfilled.

Always Reach for New Ideas. This mental stretching process is a must. This does not mean that you must promptly implement every exciting thought that comes to you, but it does mean that this attitude of always expecting to discover the pot of gold in the next idea that strikes you is an extremely valuable attitude.

The sorting process can be likened to the old miner patiently shoveling a heap of gravel into his pan and then swishing it around until the nuggets shine forth ready for his eager fingers.

This very high plane of consciousness is the pad from which most great fortunes are boosted into the multi-millionaire atmosphere of realization.

Guided Curiosity. This trait of character isn't the easiest

one to acquire. It takes guidance. However, once you have
your directional system working for you, you will think
that your career is being propelled by a million pounds
of jet thrust, so powerful is this attribute. The simple rule
that must be activated is this: "I will be curious only about
those things which are clearly for my own good, be it
growth, progress, or money.

Empathy. In recent years this word has been brought into
general use by writers and lecturers in the inspirational
field. Basically, the idea is to get readers or listeners to
think more about the other person and less about himself,
which is good, because in this manner we are able to escape the bonds of selfishness. But let's add a brand of new
thought: the idea of understanding the feelings, attitudes,
and motives of other persons for the purpose of finding
out where the trends of human interest are drifting, or
likely to explode and so get there ahead of them with the
product or service in ample supply.

Don't Blame the Other Guy, Blame Yourself. This is a
tough directive to swallow, but when the truth of this
guideline is absorbed, your forward progress will take on
so many new dimensions that you will be amazed. Why?
Simply because this is more often an excuse rather than a
bona fide reason.

Let's take a closer look. First off, when something goes
haywire with our plans the easy tendency is to blame the
result on the weather, another person, untoward events,
or an imagined conspiracy. While it is true that any one
or all of these alibis might have a grain of truth, the real
facts all point toward you as the offender.

When you are looking, planning, and thinking ahead
like a millionaire, you will be anticipating all of the contrary moves that can be made by your so-called "friendly"

contemporaries or the vagaries of nature. Or face up to the fact that you are not fully prepared for contention. Then, and then only, will you be able to see light in each of the succeeding steps. In brief, you will always be fully prepared for any eventuality, and thus be fit, mentally and physically, to cope with any act of deviousness or a normal turbulence in the weather pattern.

I once spoke along these lines to one of my classes at Alhambra Evening High School. When the period ended, a salesman approached my desk and declared, "Wow, was that an eye-opener. No more alibis for me. I am going to be the best darned salesman in the world. All this time I have been making excuses for myself for not making quota, or completing all of my calls, but no more." True to his word, this man dug in with so much will that within three months he was leading the entire sales force of his company in sales, and within eight months he was promoted to field supervisor with a smart increase in salary plus fringe benefits that he never previously believed were for him.

Learn to Ride With the Breaks. This is a skill that requires a sensitiveness to timing, an alertness to the natural rhythms of plus and minus factors in your life pattern, and the learned ability to stand up and ride when all signs are "go" for you. Any person with even an average awareness of his luck will know instinctively when things are breaking well for him. When this rhythm of events is riding high for you, be prepared.

In my own experience, I always have four or five things going for me. In preparation for these favorable times, I make written or telephone inquiries, work up proposals, or offer suggestions that will include me *in* should the idea be accepted. When I am suddenly aware that the success rhythm is about to roll, I drop everything and bear down hard on all of the plans, projects, or enterprises that I have created with the result that on more than one occasion all of my created ideas were accepted. However, even if only two or three of my plans or suggestions bear fruit, I have taken another giant step toward my goal, simply because I have learned to ride with my natural rhythms of good luck.

Since I first read A. H. Z. Carr's book on how to attract good luck, and a recent book on the subject of Biorhythm, I have passed this idea on to numerous friends and acquaintances. Persons who have accepted the idea as valid have reported fantastic success with the plan. In fact, one man who listened is well on his way to becoming a millionaire simply because he learned to ride with the breaks that came his way.

Look Beyond Today. The person who is always thinking in terms of money performs one mental exercise as a matter of habit—he looks ahead. This act of bringing the future into focus can be accomplished very easily when three reducing lenses are pulled over the rose-colored-glasses-of-unwarranted-optimism. *First*, you *estimate trends*. That is, find out where people are going so that you can take them to the selected destination. *Secondly, direct your full attention* to any and all opportunities offered you with selective curiosity, and then apply the acid test: will this move advance my career or make money for me? *Thirdly, check it out*. That is, you ask questions, discreetly of course so as not to reveal your purpose, of *all* authorities that might be able to supply you with helpful information, and never under any circumstances buy a rush act, or a high-pressure sales pitch. It is always well to remember that 999 times out of a thousand a worthwhile opportunity will wait until tomorrow.

Learn to Hold On to Your Hat. Obviously, the gesture that

is suggested is mental, but it requires balance and maturity. (This step will be fully explained in a later chapter.) When success hits big, and it will when you follow the 15 steps to riches in an orderly manner, there is all too often an uncontrollable urge to fly off in all directions.

At the moment I am thinking of the career of John Ludlow. It seems that this chap took these several discussions seriously and applied all of the steps in full force with startling results.

John was operating a small electronics shop with one helper and he was aided by his wife in the office when her services were needed. While he was a skilled craftsman, most of his work was in repair or installation. By applying the rules for selective curiosity, he one day got the idea for a little innovation that changed his life almost overnight. He applied for a patent and from that moment on, first contracts and then money flowed toward him at flood stage, but John couldn't take the sudden affluence. He fell victim to illusions of grandeur, indulged in not one but three extramarital affairs, and took to looking down his nose at former friends. In fact, he made a complete fool of himself. Before too long his wife caught on to what was taking place and promptly sued him for divorce, at the same time taking a huge chunk out of their bank account. John was jolted only briefly. He now had more time for behaving like an off-beat juvenile. Although he didn't drink more than occasionally, through his other acts of intemperance coupled with a failure to attend to business he lost control of his enterprise, and shortly thereafter he was booted out for a host of causes.

Today John is working as a skilled laborer in one of the space laboratories, a completely defeated man all because he couldn't "hold on to his hat."

Success—especially big success—is heady stuff. Only the

well-balanced can take it with any degree of equanimity; consequently, I can only urge that you apply certain disciplines and restraints to your conduct as your fortunes begin to climb—and climb they will, for such is the truth of the natural laws of increase that are now being revealed to you.

Remember that the fifteen steps that are now being spelled out for your use are not derived from the career of any one or two persons, but from the experiences and comments of many successful men and women whom I have known during the years or have had the privilege of interviewing—all of them in the top brackets of business, finance, or politics. The observations that were imparted to me were born of contention, sometimes bitter experience, and often from the vantage point of a keenly-honed hindsight.

When you have established a sound and positive attitude of expectancy, you will be adequately prepared to take the next forward step toward money-awareness. It is true that you can make it without expecting to win, but there will always be something lacking in your efforts without this essential ingredient.

Summary

1. In order to develop a true *attitude of expectancy,* a mental house-cleaning is the first order of the day. This means the mental act of booting into oblivion all hates, prejudices, fears, resentments, and superstitions.

2. Letting go of the past with its cherished memories of wrongs that have been suffered requires a fully-matured mind, and a mental stance that is aimed directly at one million dollars or more.

3. In the days of medieval chemistry, scientists worked

diligently at the task of turning base metals into gold, but in this enlightened day you possess a miracle power that is far greater than the skill so vainly sought by these early day alchemists. You possess the power to turn your thoughts into anything you want, be it gold, outstanding success, or an accomplishment of enduring value.

4. Today you can make a right-about-face and head for your first million. All you have to do is believe that you will win.

5. There are nine easy ways to counteract any mental invasion of negatives. Make them a part of your working equipment now so that you can go forward into a bright new future.

The Fifth Step
to Riches

Start Small–Grow Big
But Keep Ahead
of the Crowd

With all of the four basic principles of great accomplishment going for you, all that is needed now is to direct the full power of your selective curiosity upon the field of your interest or endeavor, and find out where the people are going. In other words, the *trend* of thinking that is just now beginning to spark an interest in your trade, business, or profession still hasn't been fanned into full flame. You can get there ahead of the crowd—providing, of course, that enough persons know where you are going, *after* you have developed a full head of steam great enough to carry you to your goal.

It is easy to learn to think, act, and become a millionaire in these United States. All you have to do is know the ground rules and you are on your way. To some persons this might sound like a poorly conceived pipe-dream, but the proof is written in the records of the Internal Revenue Service.

Today, just as for the past seventeen years, every three hours and twenty-three minutes for the full 365 days of the year, a new millionaire emerges. One of them might just as well be you.

History is replete with examples of men and women willing to contemplate the distant vistas of hoped-for achievement, but all too few of these imaginative persons attached any real significance to the first four essentials of learning to think and act like a millionaire, carefully presented for your use in these pages.

How to Develop a Practical Curiosity

The value of a *practical curiosity* as the first step to riches derives from a million shattered dreams. Many men and women with great potential vision are willing and able to step far into the future by creating ideas, but all too often they plan, invent, or devise new methods with little regard for the contemporary level of consciousness. To put it more bluntly, these persons should stop and ask themselves, "Is the average mind ready for the *big idea* that I have visualized?"

In the waning days of the fifteenth century, Leonardo da Vinci conceived a dozen or more way out innovations, including the airplane, the submarine, and the first principles of radio, but the one sticky obstacle that confronted the far-ranging genius of this man stemmed from the fact that the limited minds of his day were not prepared for his vision of the future.

To illustrate the point in another way—nearly everyone is now familiar with the sport of *surfing*. When the cry goes out, "Surf's up!" all the boys and girls come running. Human interest or response to the flow of events is very similar. And the keenly balanced surfer on the inside surge of a

great wave is comparable to the onrushing swell of enthusiasm that greets a *timely* idea. The trick, if there is one, is
to get in front of this irresistible force and go in for a successful landing.

In the early years of this century, Henry Ford sensed the
urgent want for rapid transportation. Thomas Edison realized that millions of homes abhorred the smoky grime of
candles and kerosene lamps, so he pushed the idea of an
incandescent light. William Randolph Hearst understood
the crying need of men and women to escape, even briefly,
the dull burden of commonplace lives, and so sensational
journalism was born; and Guglielmo Marconi correctly
evaluated the need for instant communications, and perfected the wireless radio, the forerunner of our present day
radio and television industry.

In other words, like the surfer, ride ahead of the *flood
of human interests* and your bank account will soon bulge
with your first million.

How to Plot Your Present Position

Within the context of these first tentative steps you will
want to know, "How do I apply these techniques to what I
am now doing, or the moves that I would like to make?"

I never cease to be amazed at the flood of information
that comes to me on call whenever I activate the thought
with intensity, and then follow it up with properly directed
inquiries. Let us begin your own quest by taking a close
look at the three basic *direction finders:* (1) Market testing,
(2) Population shifts, and (3) Trends of interest.

Each of these methods of evaluation are employed by
merchandising men with widely varying skills and all too
often a greater number of conclusions. And all from the
same set of facts. The variable here that tends to throw the

whole process out of gear is the explosive factor of human interest that is completely unpredictable. Who, for example, would ever have guessed that a plastic hoop about three feet in diameter would reach a sale of multiple millions within a very short time after it was introduced? This is precisely what happened to a toy commonly known as the *Hula Hoop*.

What inspires men, women, and children to go *nuts* over one product or device and leave another equally good item to go begging? This quirk of human nature has made millionaires overnight and ruined ten times as many hopefuls —all because of a self-induced hypnosis in matters of market potential.

To even pretend that there is one simple formula that would tend to eliminate all of the hazards of marketing would be sheer sophistry, but there are guidelines that will greatly reduce the risk of buying a pig in the poke. In order to bring these procedures into a workable plan of action it will be well to examine carefully each of the three direction finders provided for your use.

How to Test Ideas For Potential

To begin with, market testing can be applied to a small area, with limited capital outlays for advertising, product, and personnel, or it can be addressed to widely varying markets in the major metropolitan areas throughout the nation. It all depends on how much you are prepared to spend.

In my personal affairs I prefer to be cautious in giving substance to any of my big ideas. And this tendency to be restrained in my plans and projects has saved me many a badly stubbed financial toe. However, I will have to admit that this inclination isn't natural. The idea was implanted in me by the late Phoebe Apperson Hearst one day at her world-famous hacienda near the little village of Pleasanton, California. To this day I don't know what brought it on, but in a rare moment of sharing a confidence she said, "Howard, don't ever be afraid to start small."

In matters of real estate, great sprawling shopping centers, and housing developments, knowledge about population shifts is vitally important. In evaluating these mass moves of population, statistics are of some help, but there are many variables that must be reckoned with such as climate, transportation, the potential for gracious living, or just plain investment. For example, I once owned a nice chunk of property near the center of what is now Palm Springs, California, but my banker-boss didn't regard my purchase with too much enthusiasm, so I sold out for a measly fifty-dollar profit.

I am aware now that looking ahead forty years was clearly beyond my capabilities at that time, but in a gloriously souped-up hindsight I can now plainly see all of the qualities of tremendous increase.

Determining *trends of interest* requires some real mental gymnastics, with the possibility of coming up with the right findings only slightly less than capricious. The reason for this stems from the fact that so many new methods, modes and applications or extensions of our present facilities are being introduced each day that a dozen geniuses would be hard pressed to always come up with a winner, but hidden away in this mass of detail are literally hundreds of little nuggets of great value—all worth a million dollars or more. And the only way any one of them can be found is by *prospecting* endlessly. This searching process might seem tedious at times, but it can be greatly enlivened when you know that there really is a pot of gold waiting at the end of a million rainbows. Some will be misled by this apparently

fanciful idea, but there is truth here that must not be overlooked.

How to Locate Directional Finders

When you want to find where people are going, it sometimes pays to take a close look at where they have been in
the past. There are always cogent reasons why great masses
of people suddenly start moving in one direction. It could
be climatic changes, a shortage of food, a need for more
room, or a host of similar causes of unrest. The chief advantage to be derived from a study of previous shifts of
population or interests should come from a closer look at
basic causes that seem to breed a desire for change.

Nine Powerful Information Expanders

To correctly evaluate steadily building swells of interest,
or the deep undercurrents of need that bring on revolu-
tions, or reversals in thinking and attitudes, requires a constant probing for information. In order to accomplish this
search for data, or even detect straws in the wind, there are
certain well-established practices that reveal avenues to discovery that can be used by anybody with a questioning
mind.

However, it is only fair to warn you that not one single
method can be neglected if you want to step beyond the
ordinary and stride confidently into the future. I am speaking specifically of the nine *powerful information expanders*
that can lift apparently routine bits of information out of
the conventional rut of thinking. All too few persons use
these expanders, but men and women who are thinking like
millionaires employ them to the full all of the time.

I will explain these potentially explosive factors after I have provided you with the essential first movements.

Explore these fields:

1. *Libraries*—for history, references, the library index, late book releases, current magazines of recognized quality, or local newspapers in which all points of view are reviewed.

2. *Business or trade papers*—providing you are seeking specialized information about products, practices, or packaging.

3. *Your bank*—can often be the source of valuable help, but it is well to visit several if you want a *balanced* report. Bankers, and especially the chain operators, tend to think in ruts favorable to them; consequently, it pays to visit a competitor. However, if you are concerned with population trends, find out where the "biggies" are opening branches, and the direction in which they are moving. This can be a vitally important key.

4. *City Hall*—is a prime source of valuable data, if you make it a point to contact the right people. In the past, I have found my most lucrative indications of a trend not from elected officials, but from municipal employees willing to talk frankly.

5. *Census Bureau*—provides many rich sources of information. For example, should you be exploring the investment properties, you can quickly determine the growth rate of a given community by studying census figures.

6. *Chamber of Commerce*—usually has its finger on the pulse of community life, especially where business, industry, natural attractions, or special advantages are concerned. However, in this connection it is always well to know that any information you get could be *loaded* in favor of a particular point of view. This is also obviously true of the next source.

7. *Real estate operators*—conduct a business that depends entirely on commissions and the value of listings that a given operation is able to attract. Any information that you can gather here is always "suspect." The chief point to observe

here is comparison. Check all of the information you gather against other sources. The truth usually emerges in pristine clarity.

8. *Local newspapers*—have always provided me with a rich source of leads. In the past when I have contemplated a move I invariably subscribe to the local newspaper of the community which has sparked my interest as my first step. More than once this procedure has saved me from an error that could have been quite costly, or a source of discontent over an unwise move not in keeping with my wants or desires. You can get the *feel* of a community from the paper it supports. On the other hand, there is a strong plus factor. Newspapermen are usually frank and out-spoken *off the record* about local conditions, plans, or projects.

9. *On-the-spot checks*—often provide an insight into what is really going on in a given area, and occasionally will reveal previously unsuspected opportunities. For example, Ted Knowles had carefully increased his capital account until he hit the thousand-dollar-mark. One Saturday he and his wife took a trip to the high desert just prospecting. Both were interested in acquiring a piece of sand and sagebrush, strictly for investment purposes, but neither of them had any definite ideas about the immediate future.

In checking around for available property, one bewhiskered old gent let it be known that a huge retirement community was being planned and that all of the land that was needed had been purchased except his twenty-acre parcel right smack in the middle of the tract. Why this had been overlooked was not quite clear, but he suggested to Ted that he could buy it. Ted explained that he only had a thousand dollars.

"Okay, I'll take it, and your note for six months to cover the balance," the old man declared.

Ed did some fast checking and discovered the stranger's story was true, and within an hour he had taken on the apparently worthless acreage. He was risking his entire fortune.

Monday morning broke bright and clear as it usually does in the desert areas of Southern California, and all hell broke loose in the offices of the land development company. With surveyors, heavy equipment and building materials already on the way, something had to be done, but fast. Somebody "goofed" but now was no time to argue. The president of the land company was soon on his way to see Ted where he worked as a service station manager. It probably wasn't a smart move for him to go in person, but time was running out.

The first offer the high-powered executive made Ted was ridiculous, and at this point the cautious Ted realized he was in a better bargaining position than he would have dared to think at first. With figures in mind, the new land owner named a sum of $5,000 more than he had agreed originally to pay for the property, with a take-it-or-leave-it attitude. The "big shot" first exploded. Then he raved, and finally he squealed like a stuck pig, but he paid the asking price, and paid well.

From that day on, Ted and his wife became confirmed weekend lookers—or opportunity prospectors. They haven't hit their first million, but from all accounts in about five more years they will have paper and property values in excess of this amount.

The moral of this story boils down to one simple fact: You aren't thinking like a millionaire if you are sitting home watching the ball game on TV, or hiking off to feed the pari-mutuel windows in an afternoon of futile indulgence at the race track.

Why You Should Make "On the Spot" Inspections

The value of getting out in the field and talking to people cannot be overestimated. The chief point here is to always remember to *listen*—with all of the audioperceptive qualities that you possess—and with a mind that is alert to money making opportunities. There is nothing in the world that can beat the sheer excitement of hearing the thud of another big chunk of money dropping into a growing bank account.

Obviously, there are certain skills that must be in evidence as you seek out and interview persons who can impart valuable information. In fact, *first contacts* are only the initial steps on the delightful and fascinating road to riches. It is absolutely necessary that you regard every man or woman you meet as a potential million-dollar-opportunity.

There are definite *routines that* should be put in motion —not casually or without spirit—but with a real, sincere interest in the person himself and the things that are close to him, because the door you are opening into another person's life must swing on two-way hinges. What happens next should benefit him as well as you. This is a truism that is often overlooked, but it is vital to your growth and development. How to accomplish this valuable purpose will be fully spelled out for you in the next step in learning to think and act like a millionaire. You are now prepared to make your next tremendously important move.

Summary

1. The only way you can acquire a great amount of wealth, is to look ahead, plan ahead, and be there first with the most of what is wanted. Realistic offers of goods, services, or a new way of life (hope) that fill a definite need, *at the right time,* provide a royal road to great wealth or accomplishment.

2. There is no single characteristic that will get you going and keep you going like a constantly probing, practical, and selective curiosity.

3. There are three *ground rules* that must be observed when you begin to search for clues in matters of shifts, trends, and tastes.

4. In the old days, vast Mongol hordes moved toward new lands to conquer by means of a *guide wagon.* In order to return home, this rugged vehicle carried a large, crude compass that always pointed the way. In our modern search

for wealth, there are more refined practices for seeking out opportunities. When you learn the methods explained in the nine directional finders, nothing can hold you back.

5. There is nothing more valuable in prospecting for opportunities than on-the-spot-checks for information, or personal confrontation with the men and women who know the answers.

*The Sixth Step
to Riches*

How to Strike It Rich
With a Bank Account
of Contacts

The value of contacts cannot be overestimated. In fact, it is the keystone that supports the concept of growing into the preferred circle of great wealth, but even more important, the act of touching the life of another person—even briefly—in a positive and helpful manner, possesses great value. Each name that you can honestly add to your steadily developing bank account of contacts embraces the potential of *ten thousand dollars*.

Naturally enough, this reservoir of increase must be deposited in an ever-expanding resource of friends, acquaintances, and business connections. However, there is one catch to this apparently ingenious pathway to abundance. The account must be fed—at appropriate times and places—with an affirmative diet of (1) sincerity, (2) a genuine attitude of friendliness, and (3) a firm determination not to impose upon anyone within your charmed circle of friends or casual associates.

And, too, it should go without saying, all of the foregoing must be sustained with *integrity,* including mind, purpose, and action.

Throughout the years it has been my privilege to know
personally many individuals who have attained the status
of millionaires—ranging in material possessions worth from
a mere million up to a hundred million. All of these persons exemplified three vitally important characteristics,
namely: (1) A normal amount of courtesy and consideration for others, (2) Promptness in handling such routine
matters as mail, even if it were only to say, "no"; and (3)
A steadfast posture of *decisiveness* supported with a never-
ending quest for facts and/or information from *both sides*
of any situation requiring a decision.

Because it is so disarmingly easy to build a bank account
of solid gold contacts, most men and women tend to neglect
the following tremendously valuable asset, considering it
as of no consequence, when, in fact, it is the cornerstone of
all great fortunes. The trick, if there is one, is to: *listen to
everybody, but "give your tongue (promise) to few."*

From this point on, your account can achieve a daily
record of growth that is fantastic. All you have to do is
keep a private notebook or file on every new person you
meet in business, social activities, or by casual introduction.
And in this connection, the technique is not to allow your
motive to be transparent. Simply make a mental note of
basic data (a business card helps) of any information that
is offered whenever you are introduced to a new person,
without ever being obvious. The repetition here is deliberate for the very plain reason that the whole purpose of
the plan can be scuttled should you telegraph your inten-
tions.

How to Use Three Golden Words

During the course of a busy day most men and women meet several persons who are new to them. It is what each individual does with these planned, or chance meetings, that shapes his destiny. He can pass the occasion off as only important to the purpose of the moment, or he can nurture the fortuitous encounter until one day it could develop and become immensely valuable.

In order to give life and sparkle to these meetings—and this *key* is important regardless of whether the contact is new or old—it is the priceless ingredient of remembering that must be added to your planned program of increase. And by remembering, I mean the things that are of some concern to the other man or woman. For example, I have my own list of strong primary motivations which seem to animate all active persons. They are: (1) Health, (2) Success, (3) Money, (4) Recognition, and (5) Family.

To the foregoing can be added ten supporting items about each individual which should be noted—not all at once perhaps, but unobtrusively made a part of your steadily growing file of information about each person whom you have included in your bank account of contacts:

1. Birthdate, but (not age)
2. Anniversaries
3. Hobbies, if any
4. Church preference
5. Political leanings, or affiliations
6. Ambitions
7. Lodge or service club participation
8. Job or professional attitudes
9. Community enterprises
10. Interest in sports, as a participant or a fan

Actually, this practice can become one of two things: it can be a collection of so much meaningless detail, or it can bring life and vitality to the *characters* who have won a place in your bank account of contacts; and the cement that will bind them to you and your enterprises can be summarized into three golden words: *Thank you—and—Congratulations.*

Whenever a favor is extended, say "thank you," preferably in a prompt, carefully-worded note, and convey your appreciation briefly and sincerely, void of any sentimental slush. Should your contact win a promotion, achieve any special recognition, or gain an important appointment, send him an equally short note of *congratulations,* and if the knowledge of his success comes to you from a news account, include the clipping that makes mention of his accomplishment.

It must be remembered that contacts are fragile things. All of them must be handled with courtesy, understanding, and consideration, for it is known that within the area of these thoughts, you will truly be thinking like a millionaire. Now *you* can be one.

How to Put the Idea in Action

Mary Jane S. served as a school secretary in a nearby community for many years. In addition to the usual routine chores of managing a lively school office, Mary got a real kick out of remembering the birthdays of the staff and the teachers with an appropriate card. When one of them received any special recognition, had a baby, or got married, she always seemed to have the right card for the occasion. At other times when illness hit one of the group, or he lost a loved one, she was right on hand with a warm and genuine note of sympathy.

There were times during the years when Mary could have dropped the whole idea. All too many of the persons she remembered failed to appreciate what she was doing, or so it seemed. Mary wasn't looking for "gratitude" but she rightfully expected some kind of reaction or "thank you." There were always a few who would take time out to return the favor, but the real pay-off arrived with retirement day. Two surprise parties were arranged in her honor—one of them an elaborate dinner and a reception in her honor that pleased everyone to the nth degree.

On the last day of Mary's employment more than three hundred friends among the teachers, school administrators, and P-T.A. members showed up with congratulations ranging from valuable gifts, money awards, and decorations made by the students that obviously took many hours of planning, and more hours to make. The new superintendent of schools put in a surprise appearance along with some of the town fathers. Needless to say, Mary Jane S. loved every minute of "her day."

How to Reap the Rewards of Time and Patience

Contacts, or worthwhile business and social connections, are not built up in a single day. They all take time, and a lot of remembering. However, there is one bright spot in the plan. It pays off, and pays off big, if and when the idea is followed with a happy and genuine enthusiasm.

The starting point for your building program is right in your present job. And when you know the devices of remembering, information will come to you so easily you will never cease to wonder how you managed to let it pass you by. For example, while most persons are reluctant to reveal their age, very few are willing to let a birthday pass by without mentioning it.

Here is your first key. Simply make a mental note of the date and later transfer the information you have gained so unobtrusively to your file. Now for the big surprise. Next year, when the day rolls around, send the person a birthday card with a brief personal note.

The look of complete astonishment that flits over the face of the recipient is alone worth the effort, but the small token of personal recognition is secretly treasured by the person so remembered. But this is only the first step. In the life of every man or woman with whom you work there are endless opportunities to repeat this same act of apparently effortless recall. Why? Because it is a never-failing-ego-builder, and nearly always you take on a new dimension as a friend or fellow worker.

When this esteem is allowed to grow and flourish with a proper feeding of more remembrances, you will be surprised to find one day a steadily growing list of opportunities being pushed your way. It is a truism of human nature that cannot be overlooked: *People like to be appreciated, and remembered.*

Where to Find Four More Golden Keys

When I decided to become a "world famous writer," I had to admit that I knew exactly nothing about the trade. In fact, some editors with whom I deal still entertain this dastardly notion. In any event, I avidly pursued every avenue of approach that I could uncover. Of course, writers' magazines, books on writing, and the inevitable writers' club were my meat. The one big thing I did that really paid off was to make contact with famous authors. To do this effectively I was somehow guided into writing letters of appreciation for work well done, or ideas which had been discussed that were of real help to me. And did this ever pay off? Your guess is correct.

To this day, I still count among my friends men and women with whom I corresponded in those beginning days of authorship, but of most consequence to me, I always managed to edge in a query on some issue that was bugging me, and I always included a self-stamped-and-addressed envelope. This latter courtesy often went unheeded, but I know that my thoughtfulness in this matter was responsible for the prompt attention that was directed to me on more than one occasion.

Again, there is a truism in dealing with people that must never be neglected: *The bigger they are, the easier they are to reach, especially by letter, when and if you say the right thing, at the right time, in a brief and courteous manner.*

And another starting point is all too often overlooked for the reason that the low man on the totem pole of enterprise is bypassed. The lowly employee today could be the executive of tomorrow—and often he is. Try adding to your list of persons to remember the office help that presently do not seem to swing much weight. I once learned a lesson that I have never forgotten. In one of the offices that I used to visit often there was a mousey type of young lady at the reception desk. She was not likely to win any beauty awards, but she was thoroughly competent, and she did preside over all of the mail going to the editorial desk. I never failed to compliment this girl in some off-hand manner or stop briefly to josh her discreetly.

One day when I dropped into the office as usual there was a new girl at the desk. When I asked where Lindy was, the reply startled me out of my normal composure. "Oh," the new girl answered, "Lindy married the boss last weekend.'

Truthfully, I had never dreamed of any large amount of business coming from this source, but from that day on my offerings always got "top priority" in consideration, and more often than previously there were acceptances, as long as my copy was at least equal to other submissions.

The *golden keys* that you can put to good use today are these:

1. Make it a point to know the leaders in your field.

2. Make it a must to know these men and women personally if possible; if necessary find some valid reason to write to them. It can be a query, a letter of appreciation, or a *thank you* for a good idea, but do write.

3. Go back over your school-day friends and drop them a note. Most of them won't take the time to answer, but it is an odd twist of affairs to note that the ones on the way up—or on the way down—will reply. The mediocre ones you can get along without, and the ones who have missed the boat should be helped or discarded.

4. Add at least one new contact to your list every day. You can only accomplish this by getting out and meeting people, going places and asking questions. Become genuinely interested in individuals and events. Whatever is brought to your attention is worthy of examination. You never know when or where the next contact or situation will reveal a rich source of opportunities—it can be anyone from errand boy to the president.

How to Activate the Five Dynamics That Will Attract and Hold Contacts

Just as in any trade, business, or profession there are certain practices that will attract customers or clients, so is there a set of guidelines that are always followed to gain this end. Contacts are made and cemented to you in the same identical fashion. Try putting some real power into the dynamics presented here and watch your career zoom into the next orbit of success:

The Dynamic of Appreciation. This one has been touched upon lightly in a previous paragraph, but have you actually made it part of your working equipment? I would hope so. We all know that this is a trait of character which must be cultivated. A few persons learn to appreciate others early in life—especially if there are brothers and sisters to contend with during the growing up process, but even then most of us are compelled to acquire this tendency the hard way. Make it a point to show appreciation for everything that is done for you, either by the spoken word, a brief note, or a simple reaction that conveys a sincere "thank-you."

I once praised a well-known speaker for an unpopular but courageous stand he had taken on a certain issue. This man has never forgotten. Since then this person has referred more than $20,000 worth of business my way. Not a bad result for a moment of thoughtfulness.

The Dynamic of Service. Napoleon Hill, in his unusual book, THINK AND GROW RICH, describes this as "going the extra mile." This precept can be translated many ways, but the essential that we are now concerned with is how it will help us win new contacts. Boiled down to its essence, this simply means to perform little acts of extra service, over, above, and beyond the demands of your normal business relationships.

I have closely observed the careers of many successful business men, professionals, and politicians, and one quality that seems to stand out is the tendency to do a little more than the bargain calls for.

I like to recall the fledgling years of George Murphy in

motion pictures. He was always doing things for somebody. One day I asked him "Why?" His response was genuine. "I don't know, Howard, I guess I just love to do it." George Murphy is now a United States Senator and obviously headed for greater responsibilities.

The Dynamic of Consideration. There are so many practical applications of this precept I cite only three here—the ones that very easily could change the world overnight. First, if consideration for the other fellow were made a way of life, traffic fatalities would drop 90% beginning today. All that we would have to contend with would be the sheer unavoidables. Secondly, it would change politics overnight from a cheap drive for personal advantage to a high plateau of statesmanship. Thirdly, you could, by your enthusiastic acts and attitudes of consideration for your family, your associates, and your contacts, add a million dollar dimension to your total personality within a matter of days.

Realize that *your liberties end where the other fellow's begin.*

The Dynamic of Inspiration. This can be the source of fantastic good, not only for yourself, but for all of those with whom you come in contact. By word, or deed, you can spread a ray of hope—sunshine—if you will overlook the triteness of the word, a bit of badly needed courage in times of stress, or the will to pick up and start all over again. There isn't a single one of us who doesn't need this immensely valuable stimulant once in awhile. When you are at your peak, give freely, for it is precisely as a very wise man once said, "Cast your bread upon the waters: for thou shalt find it after many days."

The Dynamic of Understanding. This very special attribute of character needs to be cultivated in a way that is completely different from any of the other dynamics. To begin with, when one of your contacts is burdened with a heavy problem, or is riding high in a moment of glory, a note of sympathy, or a letter of congratulations is always in order, but the one essential ingredient that is all too often left out is the personal call, that is, actually going to see the man or woman who has been hurt, or honored. And before you go, sit down quietly and review the situation that confronts the other person, then your physical presence will have genuine meaning and vitality.

How to Find Money Value in Contacts

When I was first introduced to the potential value of *contacts* by Ed Keeler, president of Western Advertising Agency, shortly after the close of World War II, I will admit that it took me some time to assimilate the intent of such a practice.

For a while I merely kept a file card or a business card, listing pertinent information, but as time passed I began to suspect that there was a hole in the idea someplace.

One day I decided to think it out. It didn't take long. Once I made up my mind to concentrate on the problem, the answer emerged crystal clear. In later years I discovered that real millionaires had to discover the secret for themselves before they could demonstrate a big increase in money. I, too, had to learn the hard way. Simply having a file full of names possessed little value. The day the message finally penetrated my level of consciousness I began to make progress.

The *Big Idea* was to place a money value on each of my contacts. Since I wanted to be a millionaire, I knew that I would have to find, foster, and tend carefully at least *one hundred contacts*. At this point I attached an arbitrary value of $10,000 to each of my names. This added up to the one million dollars I was after, and to accomplish this, in fact, I really had to *think like a millionaire.*

As time and experience values grow, there is scarcely a week goes by that I don't add at least one name to my list, and by the same token, I often find it advisable to remove a name for one reason or another. In spite of everything, there will be casualties, but in the mainstream of affairs, and particularly yours, you will find that prospecting for new contacts is a daily must. When you have your 100 names, your holdings of money, goods, and properties will be growing all over the place, but there is one essential point that you must remember. This plan in action is a two-way-street. *You* are probably on one or more contact lists yourself; consequently, in order to *get,* you must *give.*

When your list is full, you are ready to put some real power into the next vitally important money making step.

Summary

1. Friendly, helpful contacts are as vital to your success as your practice of positive thinking, money in the bank, or your educational qualifications.

2. The three golden words that build valuable contacts and help to cement them to you are *Thank you,* and, *Congratulations,* but they must be given the power of *sincerity.*

3. In building a bank account of contacts, don't be reluctant to start at the bottom. Today's minor employee, or clerk, could be tomorrow's president.

4. It is necessary to learn, and practice, the five dynamics of human relations. These are: *Appreciation; Service* beyond the call of duty; *Consideration* for the other person; the value of *Inspiration;* and an *Understanding Heart.*

5. Put a value of $10,000 on each of your contacts, and

don't rest until you have a list of at least *one hundred*
However, it is well to remember that you will always be
faced with a recruitment problem. There will be casualties.
Remember, too, that this plan in action is a two-way-street.
You are probably on someone else's list right now. You
have to *give* in order to *get*.

*The Seventh Step
to Riches*

How to Build a Name Power
That Attracts Success

The development and directed growth of a valuable name, *yours,* that possesses real "drawing power" should be a matter of great concern to you and all other persons who would think, act, and attain the status of a "millionaire."

So much is being written these days about the *image* of a person, establishment, or locality. Let us examine the many easy plans that you can put in motion that will serve to add great value to your own "million dollar image."

When it comes to evaluating the *dynamic magnetism* that the name you bear wields over other men and women, be it one or one million, there are certain factors that must be reckoned with, or the *picture* of yourself as an effective personality will be slightly *out of focus,* or worse, completely distorted.

The Basic Qualities of "Name Power"

In order to begin this assessment of *name values,* it is essential that you regard for a moment the qualities which

are naturally a part of the *living expression* that is you as
of this very moment, for the obvious reason that it is how
you affect your friends and associates that either energizes,
or depletes, the *brand name* by which you are known.

In presenting this idea, I fully realize that many of you
will be brought up hard on a short tether. Why this should
be so is difficult for me to fathom, but it is known that even
many successful persons regard the name by which they are
identified as a lesser part of their manifestation as a human
being. When the real truth is comprehended, it is precisely
the same as the *value* you attach to the products you tend
to buy because of planned advertising. The same promotional effort that caused you to make any given purchase
in the beginning was a small *electric attraction* that awak-
ened a need within you. By the same token, you are thinking like a millionaire when you build values into the
personality that is identified by your name.

Quite obviously, you are the only one who can supply
the ingredients. You can clearly and unmistakably spell
out the person you are by your attitudes, your actions, and
your responses to the world in which you are actively engaged. In order to reach the enviable state of affairs where
you are highly, *and helpfully,* regarded by your friends and
associates, requires reasonably close attention to five very
practical steps.
These are:

1. Build and maintain a good credit rating. This can easily
be achieved by not buying beyond the limits of your income,
and paying for what you do buy or contract for *on time.*

2. Become an outstanding specialist in some field of business
—science, a trade, or a profession—and do not keep it a secret.

3. Participate in related association affairs where your acquired skills can be showcased to advantage.

4. Whenever possible, make contact with persons of responsibility who have need for the talents you have developed.

5. Constantly be on the lookout for chances to publicize your special qualities, *without being obvious.*

Planned Name Building

In addition to the foregoing suggestions, there are four more strongly positive methods, or patterns, which can be applied to building *name power*—plus one that is equally effective, but nonetheless might be considered to be negative, since it involves a risk that often skirts disaster.

1. A high spending name build-up, or publicity campaign that requires huge sums of money, plenty of highly-placed contacts, unusual initiative, and a daring disregard for all cut-and-dried name-building routines.

2. A rare, or extraordinary competence in some activity that transcends the commonplace.

3. The opportunity to perform an outstanding act of heroism.

4. The big break—that is, being at the right place at the right time, and having the skills to meet the challenge.

5. Notoriety. This one can easily be dangerous, and we do not recommend it, even as a calculated risk.

You can, without any doubt, be your own *image builder,* but the creation of a personality plus possessing the drawing power of a million magnets requires certain additives that only you can supply. How these are mixed into the end product that is *you* is entirely a personal matter, and the management of this vastly rewarding *construction project* is entirely in your hands. Others can help, providing you supply the *boosting pads* of right action, but in the end, it is you who must complete the mix in a manner that spells progress. And this forward movement must advance boldly into the future each and every day, according to the Law of Accrual.

Positive Image Building Techniques

There are many moves that any person can make that will tend to draw public attention to himself. Some of these are positive, some are creative, a few are completely neutral, and on occasion, there are some that are downright negative, if not actually calamitous. In order to avoid the confusion, even frustration, that comes with poorly conceived projects, it is well to *check out* the five main points that should guide your thinking whenever you contemplate a move that you hope will add prestige to your name. At least the substance of these guidelines should be applied to every action that you plan to activate.

1. Does the idea that I am entertaining have motive power?

2. Will it appeal to enough persons to accomplish the purpose I have in mind?

3. Can I gain any real advantage with my plan?

4. Am I inspired to make this move by my own emotional response to the idea, or because I sense a tendency of many persons to go in the direction of the action I am about to take?

5. Will the idea I am considering propel the value of my *name power* by one solid step of increase.

When to Do Something on "Spec"

As each person grows with his business plans, his career, or his profession, there will be many times when a man or woman of lesser attainments will come up with an idea, or a project that seems to possess a degree of merit. When this happens, simply go back and apply the five point pattern to the proposal. If the proposition lacks in any one of these essentials—that is, should it fail to fit neatly into every nook and corner of the form that you have just read—reject the idea promptly, and without equivocation. Any other course of action will be time wasting, energy consuming, and most certainly will add nothing to your forward movement.

On the other hand, should the idea meet all of the requirements of the guidelines, it is then time to apply the final test: *Will this idea, plan, or project advance my own program of growth, or increase my bank account in a worthwhile manner.*

When any individual reaches the stage of development where he can sit back, with detachment, and examine the essentials of any given overture, he will then, and then only, be able to bring the whole proposition into a brilliantly lighted perspective, guaranteed to ward off the devastating effects of well meaning, but impractical brainstormers.

There is always the chance that the suggestion that confronts you is valid; however, the chief concern of yours as you review the important points of the idea boils down to one vital element: *Is this for me?* If it isn't, don't be a "dog in the manger," but try and pass it on to some person among your *bank account of contacts* whom it would help. This attitude, in action, is a very strong and highly energized form of building your own name power. On the other hand, should the idea that is proffered to you possess positive, career or money building potentials, the brand name that identifies you as a person that is going places can be greatly benefited.

Nineteen Dynamic Ways to Build "Name Power"

Some of the points that I am about to present are already familiar to you, but just for the record, I am going to repeat them here so that you can use the complete list as a *check chart,* always available for ready reference until the guide-posts are firmly fixed in a habit pattern that will serve to keep you always on course.

1. Maintain a good credit rating.

2. Be extremely cautious about making promises, but keep the ones you do make.

3. Establish the reputation of being punctual, to the min-ute if possible.

4. React in a mature manner to every event, regardless of whether it is favorable, frustrating or disastrous.

5. Resolutely maintain an integrity of mind and purpose, with no deviations. If you don't know the full meaning of this word, it can be easily explained as complete honesty, restrained candor, forthrightness, sincerity and frankness, but—a note of discretion—not to the point of being rude.

6. Specialize in some practical field of endeavor that fills a real need. This requires practice, practice and more practice, leavened with a searching mind that is steadily alert for new and better methods.

7. Trade papers or professional journals offer unusual op-portunities for building *name power.* The trick here is to al-ways be on the lookout for new ideas, or combinations of old ideas. By adding a special twist of your own you have created material for an article that should be acceptable to this type of publication—even if you only raise a great big question mark.

8. Participation in civic enterprises is one sure way of getting your name in the paper, with the added benefit that often your picture will be used.

9. Within reasonable limits, service club activity will make you and your business or profession known to a large number of other business men in your community.

10. Learn how to speak coherently and effectively before an audience. This can easily be accomplished by joining your local

Toastmaster or Toastmistress Club. If there isn't one in your area, start one.

11. Be a paragraph writer. Charles Carson, well known literary consultant of Manhattan Beach, California, has built a national reputation simply by sending timely quotes, quips, and interest-compelling items to prominent columnists, radio and TV commentators, and newspaper editors.

12. Don't be afraid to send letters of thank you for favors extended or congratulations to persons who have achieved something—even if you are only slightly known to them.

13. Be a one-man newspaper clipping service. Whenever a person that is known to you wins special recognition for any reason whatsoever, clip the item from the newspaper and mail it to him. You will rarely ever be thanked for this courtesy, but your name value will increase a notch.

14. Post cards are quick and easy to write, and equally quick and easy for the recipient to read and absorb. I am acquainted with one man that always keeps a supply of cards on hand. He has his picture and name on the address side of the cards and on the top of the message side he has printed *a personal message from*—and the item that he writes is always something that might be of interest to the person receiving the card.

15. Color slide films are inexpensive and pack a real wallop when it comes to presenting you and your ideas in an effective manner.

16. Earned publicity—that is, an accomplishment that compels recognition, from newspapers and magazines, especially in the field of your enterprise—is extremely valuable. However, the one point that must be kept in mind here is that one successful performance doesn't mean you have arrived. What you have to do now is pile on a new achievement before the last one has faded from the memory of the reading public.

17. Paid publicity will do the job quickly, but it is expensive as all get-out, and extremely hazardous unless the items that are publicized about you are handled with skill and re-

straint; however, properly managed by a skilled public relations man it can build a million dollar name power.

18. The calculated risk—that is, the performance of a daring and venturesome feat—will sometimes build valuable name power over night if you are successful, but it also involves putting your name, your career and your present holdings on the line for the big try. It is like the chance roll of a pair of dice.

19. And finally, add the priceless ingredient of *quality*. There are many ways to impart the connotation of solid value to a person, a product or an enterprise, but the greatest of these derives from a judicious combination of all of the salient features of the previously described measures, aimed toward sustaining a stable million dollar character. The career of Joyce C. Hall, creator and founder of the well known line of Hallmark greeting cards provides a good example. This versatile and imaginative man insists that "People always reach up, never down, for a social custom." In support of his idea, he added a medieval type crown to the trade mark of his product. When you can accept this precept as valid, it is very easy to see how important values can be added to your *name power* by demanding that your own life pattern be molded and shaped by responsible, mature actions and attitudes, in matters of family, finance and occupation.

You Can Be Your Own "Image Builder"

The first requisite for creating an image of hard-rock dependability is to establish a record for getting things done. This basic evidence of accomplishment cannot be denied, especially when it is supported by a deliberate honesty of purpose, and sustained with an intent that is above reproach.

With the foregoing factors working for you, the next easy step is to cultivate and increase your skills every day, and nail down this picture of personal growth by finding reasonable means to *showcase* your steadily developing talents.

It is well known that a busy person is the one to turn to when you want something done capably. The man or woman who is ever alert to the favorable twists and turns of fortune is the one who will inevitably create the image of solid accomplishment, even if his actual possession of material wealth is no more than complete independence from want. However, it is well to note that this picture of an active performance sheet clearly in evidence possesses a power of attraction that is beyond all normal comprehension, so great is the force that it exerts upon your forward momentum.

The Knack of Getting Things Done

All too few persons recognize the immense power of this accomplishment factor as it relates to growth. There is a vast difference between the man or woman who is detail minded to the point of perfection, and the person who can think in the broader terms of tomorrow. While it is true that this individual might have the potential of a Michelangelo, whose attainments will be recorded in the musty corridors of history, the chances for this happening are unfortunately about a trillion to one.

Since the area of our concern at the moment involves the issue of making your name into a million-dollar attraction in the halls of business, finance, or the world of entertainment, we must pursue the more obvious, and less risky pathways to recognition. To do this effectively requires a formula that is so simple it is often overlooked. It is the plain, unadorned expedient of getting more worthwhile things done in less time. When organized and imaginative work planning is *souped up* with the powerful additive of looking ahead, your name power will take on so many new dimensions in magnetism that what you have gained will seem to defy natural law.

The one drawback to the successful operation of this plan dissolves in the wishy-washy attitude of, "I hate to toot my own horn." You either do the job yourself, or you pay a $25,000-a-year man to do the job for you. You are a far more capable person in matters of boosting your own career than is a highly paid but completely impersonal professional. Not that these skilled career building persons lack merit, or have a legitimate place in the scheme of things, but you can implement your own program of name building with (1) Very little money. (2) A few moments each day of directed thinking. (3) The push of a little action applied to the ideas that you have developed.

The techniques that will be appropriate to your particular needs will vary with each new situation, but basically, and with a reasonable regard for the dictates of common sense, keep in mind the idea that was expressed by the old Negro preacher who, when he was asked why he was so successful, declared without hesitation, "I tells 'em what I'se goin to tell 'em. I tells 'em. And then I tells 'em what I'se told 'em."

This plan in action as it relates to name building might sound like bragging, but this method can be handled with restraint, and pay off in huge benefits to the individual. Do not reveal the actual steps of your plan and you can deliver as much as, if not more than, you promise.

So let us translate the preacher's method into our own program:

1. Make it quite clear what you are going to accomplish.

2. Turn in a successful performance. That is *DO IT,* and I do mean with capital letters.

3. Then make certain that your achievement is properly publicized, and made known to the right people.

"If At First You Don't Succeed . . ."

Whoever let loose with this crusty old bromide must have had name building in mind. The reason for this belief grows out of one fact: *Solid power can be built into any name by everlastingly trying.* The name value that you create, or the total look that evolves as you, is the direct result of many small, but always consistent attempts that are aiming just a little higher that eventually brings the *big reward.* And this end result is almost inevitably true, regardless of the success, or lack of it for that matter of the ventures that you are striving to accomplish. However, if what you do try isn't a howling triumph, the total look that will eventually be you has taken on a little added luster, especially if you can accept your setback—be it large or small—with understanding and good humor. The chief issue resolves itself to one vitally important course—you must keep on trying, with this firm declaration: *This experience has taught me something. Next time I will do better.*

Find Your Niche and Settle Down Comfortably

One of the first things to be learned in science is the simple fact that water seeks its own level. Translated into the human equation we find that mind is just as irrevocably tied to natural law. We are aware that this law was known to the ancients because the venerable aphorism, "Birds of a feather flock together," has been handed down to us in one form or another through endless generations.

In the language of today we describe the condition as

levels of consciousness. What your particular level happens to be is a matter that only you can determine, but the markings of each level are unmistakable. First, and most obviously, the persons with whom you associate reflect the plane or plateau of your goals and aspirations, but whatever it is, have the guts to face up to the problem squarely, and realistically. It is the starting point of meteoric progress.

Should you find that complete fulfillment, or the attainment of great riches is beyond your present capabilities, it is far better to settle for what you can achieve than to end up in the mire of bleak frustrations. This pertinent statement, packed with power and insight, is attributed to the immortal Julius Caesar: *I would rather be the first man in a little Iberian village than the second man in Rome.*

This does not mean that you should exclude yourself from further accomplishments, but it does expose the need to be realistic about the place that you now occupy in the scheme of everyday affairs—and begin as of this moment to do something positive to further your progress, because the next step will reveal the full potential of the personality plus that is yours for the asking. All you have to do is steer your life pattern in the right direction.

Summary

1. Anyone can be his own *image builder.* All it takes is just a few minutes of thoughtful planning every day.

2. When you begin to activate the basic ingredients of name power you are adding immense new magnetic forces to your present life expression. You are also including the essential values needed to create a *personality plus* that can take you anywhere you want to go.

3. The qualities that can help you build a name value with real pulling power are in your hands this very minute,

but only you can make them a part of the total look that is you.

4. Skill in getting things done right, and on time, with as little friction as possible, is the keystone around which all other name building blocks must be fitted in order to sustain the image of success.

5. The substance of name power is derived from the act of trying. To think, plan, and accomplish new ventures, regardless of the degree of achievement, is the material from which *experience values* evolve into outstanding competence.

Why Creating a Personality Plus Helps You to Think Like a Millionaire

There is no question about the fact that the man who is creating a dynamic personality, who is going places in business, or who is amassing a fortune is continually searching for new experiences. Should there be any doubt in your mind about this statement, all you have to do is examine the records of reputable personnel agencies.

In the so-called good old days, a man with itchy feet was regarded as a drifter. This dull and unimaginative bit of propaganda was nurtured by a philosophy of management fearful of disturbing the status quo.

The Search For New Experiences

Since the end of World War II, we have been rolling ahead of an industrial expansion that borders on the fantastic. However, this tremendous upsurge of business activity has brought about a change in attitude by professional executives, the men who are going places in the new economy, that is pushing top management to buckle down to a complete re-evaluation of the old policies of hiring and retaining a staff of high level associates.

The cold facts of the situation come into perspective when it is realized that the man with deep roots in a community might be regarded as a solid citizen by his fellow townsmen. The truth of the matter is that the person who succumbs to the blandishments of staying put is also lessening his chances for advancement. But worse, he is paying a terrific price in the attributes of personality. This attitude will inevitably fail him when the chips are down in a situation that requires a high level of brain power. When a man accepts a cozy, comfortable place on the shelf, he might be making his family happy temporarily, but in the long run the cost in earnings, the chance for real accomplishment, and the draining away of magnetic energies offer little compensation for the temporary security he enjoys.

How to Jockey for Position

The executive who stays cool and loose is a fact of our economic life that must be reckoned with. He is always ready to accept the challenge of new ventures. He is always willing to take carefully calculated risks. This is not a temporary circumstance. From all accounts, we have come to accept this seeming predicament as a way of life. The prime reason for this change in attitude stems from two extremely cogent developments: first, the personal benefits that can accrue to individuals in matters of experience values; and secondly, the small world we live in. This new attitude of measuring distances in hours instead of miles is quite disconcerting to the person who thinks in ruts, but the up-and-coming, strictly mobile man or woman now regards the world and, perhaps as close as tomorrow, outer space as his or her oyster.

Try Opening a New Door Every Day

There are many factors that contribute something of value to a million-dollar level of consciousness. In an earlier chapter we described the first requisite as a *money-consciousness*. Without this vital ingredient, hard work, education, a broad knowledge of your trade or profession, or the sometimes elusive circumstance of good luck will be of little help in attaining the high plateau of a millionaire mentality. How to edge into this preferred circle of awareness depends entirely upon your ability to focus all of your native skills, mind powers, and special abilities into one highly energized but carefully managed drive for success.

You can begin by opening new doors, experiment with doing things differently, being confident enough of your basic aptitudes to reach just a little beyond your present capacities, and be ever alert to opportunities that are all too often explained as sheer luck. Your hand should always be reaching out for new doors to open.

You Can Move With the Tides of Fortune

To accomplish this extending practice effectively requires only the guidance of three little words: *aim, intent, responsibility*.

When the full meaning and significance of these words are fused into one forward-moving purpose, the resolve, if it is firm and undeviating, tends to establish the aura of a man who is going places. This far-ranging attitude on the part of his employees has caused many a top executive to regard his costs sheets with a malevolent eye, forgetting to look for cause in the flamboyant but rarely-fulfilled retirement plans of his company. In fact, these very same companies exert steadily mounting pressures on a man to get him to quit when he is within two or three years of achieving the comfortable retirement that he was promised when he was a young man. As word spreads among the hired help that these promises are just so much hot air, the big move is on.

Actually, this has proved a tremendous boon to American business for many reasons. First and foremost, however, this awakening on the part of rising managerial talent has not only greatly improved the caliber of executive control, but it has literally dynamited top-level administrators out of the static attitudes that prevailed up until the late, lamentable great depression.

The result of this surging upheaval has been to create a whole new breed of men charged with a dynamic form of executive responsibility. In the beginning the medicine was bitter, but as the old tycoon types began to retire or pass on, a bright new level of men and management began moving in to take the place of the old, stately, static poses of the top brass.

How Long Is Enough?

To fill this current need for movement, many flourishing enterprises make a business of marketing top-level experience values. I am informed that a tour of duty in any one plant or operation for longer than three years involves this risk of stagnation.

The military discovered this profound secret long ago, but it took the hired help almost a century to catch up with this obscure truth of natural law. Now, nearly all levels of management are on the move, with personal attributes of personality, depth of experience values, and steadily expanding skills proving to be a tremendous source of personal satisfaction.

All of the things that have been brought out and spotlighted for your consideration in this chapter are part of the highly desirable and steadily expanding personality plus. It is a legitimate part of the package that stimulates a man or woman to *think like a millionaire,* simply because this whole attitude tends to create an awareness of opportunity, regardless of the number of horizons that must be seen, reached, and passed, in order to gain ever greater vistas of accomplishment. It may not be the proverbial pot of gold waiting for you, but most assuredly you have established the principle of growth within yourself. You will never vegetate in any one job or locality, no matter the blandishments of a somewhat dubious promise of security.

A Rolling Stone Gathers Money

In the gladly forgotten good old days, we had some really classic bromides pushed off on us as pearls of wisdom: for example, "a rolling stone gathers no moss." Without question these trite observations were dreamed up and extolled as fundamental truths by a management too lazy, or worse, too incompetent to function in an atmosphere of progress. In this connection I am always reminded of the career of Jack Matson. This chap worked for twelve long years in the production end of a paper box factory. By the slow process of attrition within the ranks of the mill hands, Matson finally was made supervisor of the manufacturing end of the business. In the meantime he had acquired a sound working knowledge of the paper converting business, so much so that one day he decided he wanted a better deal for himself and his family and asked for an outside sales job. He was refused. Undaunted, he quit on the spot, and moved bag, baggage and family to San Francisco. When he was settled he condensed all of his experience values into two pages of carefully prepared typewritten copy and went to a small paper box factory in the Bay area. The head of the firm was impressed enough with his apparent capabilities to hire him and, to test his mettle, assigned him to the roughest territory the company was trying to cover.

If I ever saw a personality blossom, this one really began to shine. In fact, it would be nearer right to say that his whole being *erupted*.

Almost from the very beginning Matson turned in an enviable sales record, so much so that within a very short time he was made sales manager, and his earnings were more than double what he had been making in his factory job.

In his production work his social standing was about what any factory hand would expect, but in his new assignment he was soon welcomed into an exclusive country club. And because he was a quiet, purposeful character, he was soon hob-nobbing with many of San Francisco's established business executives.

Once again it had been made devastatingly clear to me that another proverbial myth had been exploded: "A prophet is without honor in his own country." A *change* can bring out facets of personality and skills previously either submerged, or often more lamentably, unrecognized by those men charged with running the company.

Intensity Is the Measure of Desire

Wanting to achieve or accomplish something with intensity is not only the first step to riches, it is also the only self-activated energy that can put real fire-power into the manifestation we portray as personality. This force of attraction begins with wanting to grow and expand in body, mind, and spirit so much that it vibrates the whole being, but it is given a thrust of energy so great that it cannot be measured when it is strengthened by a normal interest in the opposite sex.

Once money-consciousness has become part of the personal complex, it is well to be unmistakably clear on one point: sex is only one of five of the driving powers that tend to forge a highly energized personality. Other factors that must be accepted as important are: money—power—prestige—and achievement. The only reason I am compelled to give first place to this primal urge derives from the fact that it is the second law of nature and therefore takes precedence over the remaining four in the scheme of things.

Since our main purpose here is to start you on the road to a dynamic and favorably magnetized personality and a steadily improving dominance over any and all situations with which you are confronted, let us now examine the five basic steps that must be considered as they relate to you and your forward progress.

To begin with, the supporting characteristic that must be energized is intensity. This is nothing more than a strongly directed attention. It is like blowing on a small flame in order to intensify the heat. It puts fire in the interest you direct toward a given subject. When this is accomplished, enthusiasm for your project begins to grow as if prodded by all the powers of the Universe.

In order to reach this first plateau of awareness, it is necessary for you to recognize and give meaning to the high vibrational level of energy that you have created. When this source of power is tapped, be ready to skim off all the idea values that are revealed to you.

Should you entertain the notion for a single instant that this declaration is sheer fantasy, you are challenged to give full meaning to the following five guidelines. You will quickly discover that you are creating within yourself all of the positive forces that will take you anywhere you want to go.

1. Single out and direct an intense but restrained interest toward one member of the opposite sex—even if you are married; in that case, however, be sure to keep the intensity within the family circle. Not only will you be creating a new and vigorous million dollar personality, but you will be bringing together all of the elements of a second honeymoon.

2. Generate an intense appreciation of the capabilities, accomplishments or goals of the man or woman in your life. Always make it a point to acknowledge with sincere thanks any little favors that are performed for you. Always be handy with a valid compliment in matters of dress or appearance; in fact, any effort made by the object of your attentions beyond the call of duty should be recognized with a favorable word. These little gestures will not only tend to raise your own vibrational level to new plateaus of magnetism, but they will serve as a tremendous morale booster to the other person. When this happens you have created for yourself a higher plane of intensity from which to launch your next planned step toward the preferred circle of millionaires.

3. Cultivate an intense but quiet and well-modulated voice. A loud, boisterous or uncouth voice scatters the natural attraction of personality in all directions.

4. Create an intense desire to grow, to expand, and to accomplish something worthwhile. This new achievement does not necessarily need to be work-connected. It can be any one of your extracurricular activities just so long as your interests are positive. It is often quite surprising how much personal magnetism can be increased simply by being elected president of your church board, civic group, or service club. With each new level of advancement that is attained, fresh sources of power

and authority add some degree of luster to the life expression that is yours—especially when you handle your new eminence with poise and discretion.

5. Proceed with an intense desire to be independent. At this stage of our discussion you might rightfully ask, "What does this have to do with thinking like a millionaire?" Well, the plain, unadulterated facts are these: unless and until you are able to intelligently and unselfishly sever all dependent connections with mama or papa, overly zealous governmental agencies except in situations of dire emergency, you are not thinking at your highest level of efficiency and you have opened up a hole in the dike of riches that could easily drain away all of your positive mind values in a matter of hours.

On the surface this declaration might appear to be just a little too much for some persons, but when the full truth is comprehended, dependence in any form—to humor either a parent or your own sense of insecurity—tends to weaken the moral fibre, dissolve integrity of mind and greatly lessen the essential quality of self reliance which, after all, is the key characteristic needed to think in high gear.

Ten Sustaining Pillars of a Powerful and Magnetic Personality

In addition to a carefully-managed sex interest there are ten more factors that upgrade the potential of a highly energized force of personal attraction. Some of these might appear to be just too commonplace to even consider, but when you bring the whole ball of wax into clear perspective, the several old-hat ideas offered for your consideration are not quite so ordinary after all. For example, the first item on our list of supportive measures is *water*. Out of instinctive habit, all of us accept water as a matter of course for the usual purposes of drinking, cooking, washing and bathing. Now let us consider for a moment that water also cleanses from the inside—and when we fail to drink enough of it to perform this essential function, the whole body mechanism begins to lag in efficiency with a consequent decrease in the powers of personal magnetism. Thus it is imperative that you make it a habit to drink from six to eight glasses of pure, clean water free of ad ditives every day—more, if it is needed.

Nutrition. It is impossible to repeat too often that what we eat can make us come alive. Odd quirks and tastes for certain foods, as well as odd-ball eating habits, can drain off the forces of attraction faster than these energies can be created by even the most powerful of directed mind powers. The rule: Sit down quietly three tims a day to a balanced assortment of fruits, vegetables, and proteins. If you aren't sure of your body requirements, consult your family doctor, or a reputable dietician free of any food faddist ideas.

Rest. Why this essential body requirement should have to be emphasized is difficult to understand. All too many men and women fall by the wayside simply because this part of the daily routine was neglected, or worse, aborted. The simple rule here is: when you are tired, take a nap or go to bed for a full night's sleep. Only urgent necessity should be cause enough to vary this practice.

Enthusiasm. Here we go again with another of those ad- monitions that seem to dull with each repetition. Take just a moment to evaluate the fact that personal magnetism is based upon the first three items on our list, but it is only brought into a full and highly energized force when it is triggered with an intensity of interest which we describe as enthusiasm. This desirable state of mind simply means to get reasonably excited about something and stay that way, *with restraint.* This is the catalyst that fuses the whole personality into what we often characterize as a *fire-ball*. This description could fit you, providing you give strength of purpose to the next item on our list.

Project. This is a trait that has to be learned and constantly energized. Recently, in the Miss Hawaii Beauty Contest Finals in Honolulu, I watched a very lovely and extremely photogenic girl take third place, simply because she had never learned to PROJECT her personality farther than arm's length. This may have been sufficient for holding purposes, but this delightful female learned on this occasion the hard way that she couldn't project herself beyond the bright footlights. This knack of extending an *outgoing* personality can be cultivated so easily, but it must be implemented by the next item on our list.

A Sense of Humor. To frown requires the concentrated use of every muscle in the face, but to grin, just turn up the corners of your mouth and relax. When this is accomplished the whole environment takes on a rosier hue. From this point to the next is an easy turn of the mind—from negatives to positives. Since it demands the direct employment of all facial muscles to look grim, you can say quite truthfully that every body cell is in energy-depleting confusion when you are downcast or your attitude is negative. In order to offset this devastating influence, always be ready with a timely quip, a bright response, or a word of honest encouragement (without sickly platitudes) regardless of the source of upset.

How to Put the Keystones of Personality in Place. Now we come to the place in our construction enterprise of creating a vibrant personality where we have to put the *keystones* in place in order to hold the entire structure intact. First of these essentials is a strong, balanced interest. In practice, this means that we share in proportion to cause an intense and directed attention to all the values that can be derived from work, recreation, entertainment and cultural pursuits. Without this *revved up* intensity of purpose, much of the pulsating spark of personal magnetism can be lost, or worse, frittered away. However, should we lack in this important part of our total personality, it will be difficult to animate with any degree of success the next step of our planned program of growth.

Cultural Attainments. This does not mean that you must cultivate a special aptitude for art, music, poetry or classic literature, but it does mean that an ardent regard for these cultural advantages be made a part of the *You* that is being slowly forged into a dynamic personality.

Special Skills. Now we come to a new and exciting plateau wherein we begin to concentrate on the constant rehearsal of one special skill until one day we come to be recognized as the *world's greatest.* When you have implemented all of the foregoing sustaining factors of a *personality plus,* you are ready for the tenth, and final step.

Socializing. This means entering into group activities of any nature wherein men and women meet together for purposes of fun and relaxation. This can be a dance, a special kind of party, a show-off tea, a charity benefit, or a cultural recital. The main concern here should be conviviality in all of its positive aspects. The exchange of pleasantries, meeting new personalities, participating in games that tend to relax—all of these things are simply additional catalysts that help to form a positive, vibrant and attractive human expression with strong magnetic energies.

In the next step we will explore one unusual phase of a high potential of the millionaire thinking process that is too often skipped over as unimportant, but when the truth is known, it can be as explosive as a firecracker in a barrel of gasoline. You can make this exceptional skill part of your money-making bag of tricks today.

Summary

1. There is no doubt that a well-managed sex interest plays a vitally important part in bringing power to an emerging personality plus.

2. An attitude of controlled intensity can create a dynamic physical magnetism that will serve to raise any man or woman above the commonplace.

3. Cultural attainments can add immeasurably to the powers of attraction of any man or woman, when they are kept in balance with other basic factors of personality.

4. The person who thinks, works, and plans, even casually, for a chance to improve himself has included a powerful additive to his total expression.

5. It is becoming far more apparent every day that the person who plays it cool and loose stands a far better chance of achieving success than the man or woman content to *stay put* in a hum-drum job that lacks rewarding challenges for growth and increased responsibilities. To be afraid of change is to risk failure to move with the tides of fortune

How to Develop the Courage to Think Like a Millionaire

Stepping out ahead of the field in any line of endeavor with the idea of achieving great success, requires not only raw courage, but it also involves all of the other attributes of being that are included in the sum total of thinking like a millionaire. In fact, all fifteen steps must be implemented in full force and absolute quality. In other words, each of the directives that are explained in Step Five must be built up and highly energized by all of the essential traits of character, in full support of the advantages that are offered by *natural law*.

It Takes Guts to Be a Pioneer

When we were kids, Jimmy Doolittle, normally a reticent chap, told me that he was determined to be an aviator. This was a true pioneer speaking, because flying in those days was scarcely the safest venture in the world. I was reminded of his emphatic declaration when I heard the news that General James Doolittle had taken a group of intrepid flyers on an extremely dangerous mission over Toyko in World War II.

On another occasion, a high school friend informed me one day that he was going to quit school. We were then in the tenth grade. He wanted to homestead in the high desert country of Indian Wells Valley. Not having my "rose-colored glasses" on at the time, I failed to see anything but vast stretches of sand and sagebrush. Time passed on and the little village of Inyokern woke up one day to find *Harvey Field,* forerunner of the sprawling Naval Ordnance Test Station at China Lake, practically in their front yard. My friend the dropout was ready. In the intervening years he had bought up every piece of land he could get his hands on, purchased the only store in town on borrowed money, taken on the job of Postmaster, bid in the distributorship of a major oil company, and established a trailer park complete with needed facilities. Naturally, all of this foresight paid off big, simply because he acted with courage. When he retired recently he was sitting solidly in the lap of comfortable abundance.

It does take *guts* to be a millionaire—to step out in front of the parade, especially when you aren't sure of the route the procession is going to take. However, in the sweeping look you direct toward all of the variables before you take action, you will gain perspective. You are thinking like a millionaire when you weigh the risks against possible benefits before you step off into the void of tomorrow, but only after you have lined up a solid phalanx of facts to support the move you are planning.

I am certain that my high school dropout friend fully realized the hazards of his venture into rugged desert country and that Jimmy Doolittle knew the moment he left the ground that he was at the mercy of the law of gravity and only sustained in the air by a man-made machine that was, at best, a contraption of doubtful quality in those early days of flying; nonetheless, both of these men made their moves with a full belief in themselves. Both of these men won mightily. The first acquired a comfortable fortune, and the second not only earned his million, but also found a secure place in history.

How to Know the Seven Dynamics of Courage

There are seven vitally important characteristics that compose the sum total of a really courageous man or woman. All you have to do is try and fit this outline over your present life pattern and you will promptly know the extent of your fearlessness—and precisely how much programming you will have to accomplish before you are truly thinking like a millionaire.

The *first* essential is a completely detached but nonetheless probing point of view. In other words, an unrelenting search for facts should guide your every move.

The *second* essential is to know how to weigh and compare all advantages and disadvantages of every move that you contemplate.

The *third* essential is to escape the sticky bonds of wavering, or hesitation, once you have reached a conclusion, based upon information derived from the first two qualities.

The *fourth* essential is to learn how to evaluate trends in human interest. For this purpose try a judicious reading of such publications as the *Wall Street Journal,* or the *U.S. News and World Report.* Syndicated commentators will be of great help but only if you are also willing to read established representatives of the extreme right, the extreme left, and the poised middlegrounders This is the only method presently known that will give you a fully balanced outlook on coming events.

The *fifth* essential is to create and maintain a *risk capital* account, be it $5.00 or $5,000,000—the principle is the same. This is a must. In brief, everlastingly be looking for "Miss Opportunity"—and don't be always waiting for her to knock—the old girl has a lot of doorbells to ring.

The *sixth* essential is to learn the validity of one single economic fact of life: *Never hesitate to sell or negotiate a deal if you will make a profit.* Many disillusioned men and women have learned the hard way that waiting for the *big killing* is no different than looking for the end of the rainbow.

The *seventh* essential is to cultivate and sustain one basic trait of character: Never stop to count your gains or losses. Forward movement is the only energy that should be applied to your never-ending quest for growth, regardless of whether it is mind or millions.

Why It Takes Courage to Adjust to the Millionaire Consciousness

Did I say that it took courage to implement, and sustain a million dollar consciousness? This is probably an understatement of fact that will do for a long time to come. I am thinking of five men and one woman, each of whom is fortunate enough to be in the favored group of millionaires —class of 1968. Two of these persons are following the principles of growth that I am enunciating for your use now. Their fortunes are growing slowly but surely. The remaining four, all men, are sitting complacently, if not fearfully, upon their holdings, afraid to grow—wasting time bemoaning the evils of our tax system, the changing times, and the unmistakable, never-ending blunders of our elected officials. The mental stagnation that has overtaken these otherwise brilliant men borders on the pathetic.

Years ago I persuaded one of my acquaintances—a reluctant millionaire—to begin moving into the bright hours of tomorrow *one day at a time*. At first he debated the advisability of setting aside even $25.00 of risk capital. This was understandably a real venture for him, but once this man got his feet wet in the waves of the future there was no stopping him. Now he is a happy, purposeful man, eager for new opportunities and, most important of all, he is no longer sitting on his eggs of fortune like an expectant mother hen.

Create an Aura of Courage—It Is Protective Cover

There is one characteristic that is forever clear in the manifestation of a courageous person. It is a certain "something" that seems to surround him as a shield against false pressures, the cares and burdens of the hour, or the blandishments of the "big deal that must be accepted right this minute or it will be lost forever." Remember this: *There is no legitimate offer that won't be just as open tomorrow as it is today.*

When this appearance of a *solid rock* is presented to the world, a front that can only be moved by hard facts, it tends to impart and sustain a genuine pose of incisiveness that cannot be moved by shallow argument. And further, it is a powerfully sustaining factor in the highly desirable quality of decisiveness that we must build toward, and achieve, in the fifteenth step.

You Can Create Your Own Shield

In addition to the seven dynamics of courage that must first be implemented with strong determination, there are three additional attitudes that should be made a part of the total personality. As you begin to absorb the basic causes that create a million-dollar level of consciousness, you will find these suggested traits of character repeated in several different ways as you confidently take each new step toward wealth, mental awareness, and spiritual discernment. This is done deliberately and with a purpose. It is like fitting the pieces of a jigsaw puzzle together. Each special nuance of application will eventually fall into place, and you will know you have it made.

The three mental moves can best be summed up as follows:

1. If it needs to be done, do it now—or at the very earliest opportunity. Like the high-powered racer hurtling along a speedway at an incredible pace—watch your chance and make the reluctant duty an accomplishment.

2. Resist with courage and forthrightness any high pressure pitch that demands a quick take-it-or-leave-it decision. In this connection, it is well to note that all *big deal* salesmen employ this technique with a hundred variations.

3. When the total facts are in, sort them out, reach a conclusion, give it real fire-power with a *yes* or *no* judgment, and then stick to your guns with no deviations.

Courage comes in a wide variety of shapes and sizes, and it is expressed in just as wide an assortment of performances.

However, it is only right that we should know that in venturing far beyond the limits of ordinary caution, undying fame, and sometimes a fantastic increase in wealth, can be gained.

I remember well talking to the late R. Anderson Jardine, the little Bishop who staked his life, his career as a man of the cloth, and his meager fortune in support of his right to act according to the dictates of his conscience when he stepped forward as the only member of the Anglican ministry who would marry the Duke of Windsor to Wally Warfield Simpson. When I asked him why he did it, he simply said, "Howard, I knew it was right."

"How?" I inquired.

"Because I thought about it for days on end, and then I prayed." And his declaration was so unpretentious, I knew then his niche in history was cut from solid rock.

In later years I was always reminded of his simple statement whenever I received a note from him. His brief but cheery comments about his affairs would conclude with "Best wishes *and prayers* of the Bishop."

I'm reminded of another occasion when I failed in courage and was subjected to well-deserved reproach. I was talking to a group of prominent writers in a general meeting of *The Manuscripters* shortly after I had consented to the removal of an extremely provocative statement I had made in my book, *"How to Create the Big Idea."* In my talk I tried to explain why I had agreed to make the deletion, although I suspect my defense was rather weak. At the conclusion of the meeting, Stella Terrill Mann, author of the now famous classic *Change Your Life Through Prayer* came up to me and with a look which I am sure spelled more than disappointment, said, "Howard, you should always have the courage to say what is right. Never hesitate to tell all you know when you are sure of your position."

Several years later I had urgent cause to remember Mrs. Mann's words. Five major magazines during the course of a two-year period came out with strong, colorful stories, supported by sound scientific findings, in which proof of the belief that I had chosen to scuttle was offered as positive fact. Had I possessed the courage at the time to stand up for my concepts, I would have profited greatly.

The only point of restraint that I would suggest here is this: Whenever you step outside of popular beliefs, regardless of whether they are biblical, political, or economic, be absolutely certain of your facts. To go off half-cocked over some poorly-conceived notion can mean nothing but sheer disaster.

How to Know the Quality of Courage

Long ago the venerable Confucius observed, "To see what is right and not do it is want of courage."

So far, all of the steps provided for your use in learning to think like a millionaire are the sturdy foundations and framework of the mental traits you need to cultivate in order to reach a state of affluence. From this point on your very special construction project must add important and absolutely indispensable characteristics to the sum total of your life expression. In other words, now is the time for you to bear down and give substance to the essential qualities that tend to help you acquire and retain great wealth.

It takes courage to resist temptation, to fly in the face of convention, to be a non-conformist, not in a *kooky* sense, but rather in attitudes. For example, trying to keep up with the Joneses, whoever they may be, is not only immature, but it shows a distinct lack of self-reliance, and self-reliance is, without question, the basic sustaining factor in pure white courage.

There are many facets to the quality of courage, but the one you are mostly concerned with here is a strong and unrelenting determination to grow a little every day, not only in wealth, mind power, and physical vigor, but also in a strong inclination to include a spiritual leavening of the whole manifestation that is your life expression. On this latter point, it is suggested that you do not include a cultivation of purely religious indulgences, which all too often is nothing more than a doubtfully pious prayer, without meaning, or worse, mere lip service to the pomp and ceremonies of religion. Most emphatically, however, you should know the special attributes of being that can sense the spiritual qualities of the God-concept in a symphony, great literature, the quiet beauties of nature, or the outward revelation of character in a truly courageous person. These are the things that will place you in tune with the miracle powers of Infinite Mind.

How to Offset the Variables of Chance

It takes courage to step off into the future with any degree of confidence. To offset the possible diversities of chance, there is one factor that should always be considered. This is a matter of *timing*. In the next step you will learn to know the value of time, and timing in planning your ventures into the variables that can always come when you open the door on tomorrow ahead of the crowd.

Summary

1. There are many facets to the quality of courage, but the one we are concerned with here is the determination to grow a little every day in money, mind power, and physical vigor.

2. The seven dynamics of courage must be kept alive and vibrant all the time if we want to grow in consciousness.

3. It requires real courage and fortitude to adjust to the millionaire plateau of thinking and acting.

4. When you create an aura of courage you have pro-

vided yourself with a protective shield that is virtually impregnable by any untoward event.

5. It takes *guts* to be a pioneer, but it is one of the few ways to think or act that tends to produce a high level of money oriented plans.

The Tenth Step
to Riches

How to Manage Time
to Make It Pay
Big Money

Your first big move is to organize yourself. Before anyone can plan his time-use efficiently, it is necessary for him to fully adjust himself to a money consciousness. On the face of it this might seem to be an unnecessary directive, but when we stop to take a second look, the truth emerges in primal clarity.

Let us take a moment to examine the career of Jim Dutton. It seems that Jim had worked himself into a comfortable job in one of the giant aircraft plants. His educational background was only about average, or perhaps a little less, since he hadn't finished his last year in high school. He had married young, perhaps earlier than he should have, but now that there were four young Duttons to care for, the course of his life followed a commonplace routine—home at five in the evening, a hectic meal with the family, a TV program or two, with everyone yelling for a different station, a phone call here and there from associates or family and then to bed by ten o'clock.

Sounds pretty dull, doesn't it?

Apparently this same thought struck Jim one day because his whole life changed overnight. Where to start was his only problem. This was quickly solved for him. His department head always managed to keep an impressive array of recent business books on his desk. One of these was *How to be a Better Supervisor*. Jim asked if he could borrow the book for a few days. Without a word it was handed to him. Reading at home with all the family commotion was a real exercise in restraint, but he solved this situation by going into the bathroom and shutting the door, since this seemed the only privacy he could command.

Within a week he was back with the book and asked for another one. This time the manager handed Jim a stiff one, *Problems in Management,* and even though it was half in jest, he accepted the challenge. In one of the chapters of the new book was a complete discussion of time management, and in this section was one hard-hitting statement that got under his skin: "Sound time management begins with the degree of skill that you use to control your off-duty time."

Jim took this to heart, and within a week he was devoting an hour or more each evening to reading everything he could get his hands on pertaining to the aircraft industry, *and planning his work flow at the factory.*

Within a short time, the output of work in Jim's little section was increasing way beyond the norms. Naturally, this kind of effort wasn't long in coming to the attention of the supervisor. But this worthy chap had a tiny streak of insecurity in him. The only way he could think was that Jim was after his job. There was, in his limited reasoning processes, only one thing to do—unload Jim on one of the other supervisors. This was accomplished easily, since the person he selected for the honor was on the lookout for a good man.

As it turned out, in the new job Jim's tendency to plan his work carefully was not only recognized, but appreciated. Within a short time the supervisor was promoted to department head and Jim was made supervisor. But—the big surprise came a year later when the department head moved into a vice presidency and Jim moved into his office —and all because he began to plan his personal time and extended this idea into his daily work.

Perhaps this sounds like an oversimplification of "how to succeed in business without really trying," but the truth is that so few persons actually plan personal time schedules that there is virtually no competition.

The Seven Basic "Use of Time" Plans That Can Change Your Life Overnight

You might regard a personal inventory of time-uses as just too much work, but you can bring this chore into quick perspective if you will simply regard each move you make as a step in the direction of great wealth, accomplishment, or a coveted promotion.

There is always the chance that your plans will fail to blossom with rewards until you begin to apply realistic "testing" procedures. First try these guidelines on your daily work output for size—and if only one or two fit your particular situation you will not only be really thinking like a millionaire, you will be laying the groundwork for an unusual success story—yours.

Top Priorities. Plenty has been written and said about the subject of *priorities,* but the real test insofar as you are

concerned boils down to this: Does the time I am allotting
to this project mean money to me now? There is simply
no other criterion that applies in this instance.

The Establishment of Work Goals. Oddly enough, no one
grows in mind, muscle, or money until easily achieved
work goals are written down, and stabilized as a permanent
part of the planned program of increase.

The Daily Growth Pattern. Every minute of every day
allotted to your work schedule should be used to create a
richer you. To accomplish this purpose effectively requires
that you correctly assign to the time periods under your
control the building blocks of *increment,* both earned and
unearned. The first part of this increase should come from
payment for your services today, and the second should
come from making smart moves, wise investments, and
anticipating the flow of human interests.

Planning Time Schedules To Reduce Waste Effort. This
one is a real toughy, but if a person will start with the
obvious time wasters, it won't be long until he will be
anticipating the intrusion of unproductive moments and
be prepared with alternate courses of action. While it is
true that not all of the fill-ins you devise will fit the situation that confronts you, there is one thing for sure—you
will have added from one to several strong daily pushes to
your forward movement, instead of coddling a costly time
loss.

Learn To Roll With the Punches. Without question there
will be unforeseen events that will disturb the best laid
plans you can devise, but the smart operator takes them in
stride, picks up the badly scattered pieces of time, and
tries to salvage some gain from them, even if it is only a

powerful affirmation like "something good will come of this."

How to Set Realistic "Deadlines" For Performance. In the beginning, there will be a tendency to stretch too far, reach too high, or plan too much. The cure for this is within easy reach. Simply take the hours, days, or weeks, that you have assigned yourself for the completion of your plan or project and divide the total into patterns of daily accomplishment. That is, make it an unrelenting point to take X number of steps toward your goal during the period of time that you have assigned yourself—and, if possible, exceed this increase, be it ever so small.

How to Be Your Own "Organization and Methods" Engineer. This step is so easy it is a never failing cause to wonder why it is often overlooked. Perhaps the mere simplicity of the idea pushes it clear out of focus. In order to apply the factual approach to your program, there are seven courses of action open to you. When these are implemented to the full extent of their potential, you are on your way. Let us begin with your daily work schedule.

1. The work day. This means the number of hours you plan to work on any given day, be it two, four, or ten.

2. Plan your creative work for the times when you are most creative, regardless of whether it is morning, noon, or midnight.

3. Go over your plans for the day and cross off the items that do not spell growth, prestige, or money.

4. Match the moves for similarities, such as area, community, or territory so that there will be no duplication of travel time, effort, or ventures. Then combine the remaining items into a productive unit of progressive performance.

5. There will be times when you will have to alter or limit your planned moves for many reasons. When this happens, it is

well to always have something to replace the item on your list that has failed to come through as expected.

6. In merchandising there is an old slogan that says "We never substitute" but in time planning it is a must. Emergencies will erupt, appointments will be voided, decisions will be changed, or an impossible spell of weather might intrude. When this happens, always have an alternate course of action ready for use.

7. Learn to intersperse routine chores in time lags that can't be avoided, or at a time of day when energies are at low ebb.

The Money Needs of Today—and Tomorrow

When you are planning the money-making needs of today, do not neglect the equally important time values of planning for tomorrow. By all means, project your aims, accomplishment-goals, and ambitions into the future. To do this effectively, and in a manner that is stimulating as well as imaginative, make certain that each and every step of the way is covered by a challenge to your present capabilities.

This need for stretching skills, talents, and competence beyond the achievements of today is nothing more than taking advantage of a powerful natural law that will work with you in a most rewarding manner whenever you invoke its full potential. The strategy here is to always aim just a little higher than the point of excellence that you now enjoy.

The Six Positive Factors of Time—
and a Word of Caution

There are six variations of the word, "time" that must be reckoned with in preparing a daily schedule, or a program of growth that is realistic. Since the real meaning of these variants are all too often overlooked, it might be well to spell them out for you, together with comments that should be helpful in relating them to your own plans and enterprises:

Timing. Ask yourself: "Is what I am now initiating right for me now?" "If I should put steam behind this move would it serve my best interests?" "Would it integrate with my other plans and give them a forward boost?"

Timeless. Ask yourself: "Would what I have in mind be good today, tomorrow, or next year?" In other words, is your contemplated move so basic in the human scheme of things that it doesn't need to be fully implemented today?

Timely. This is close to, but not exactly similar to timing. The variation derives from the fact that what you have considered as a smart move today must fit in with the trends of public interest. You should watch this one closely because it could really derail your plans and purposes if this important factor were not fully evaluated.

Time-serving. The question to ask yourself here is this: "By making this move am I spending my time to the greatest possible advantage?" When any project comes under the close scrutiny of this question, you will quite often discover that your idea has more holes than a sieve.

Time. As determined by a term in office. This is the period of time which has been allotted to you by an election, or appointment, to show what you can do. When your time is planned with purpose, imagination and efficiency, you can prove that you are capable of larger responsibilities. This is the one big chance that most politicians and office holders neglect in favor of the social prestige and emoluments of office.

Pertinence. This means being at the right place, at the right time, and fully prepared for the big opportunity. I am reminded of the story of the GI in Japan who wrote his girlfriend back home that he was "going with" a native girl. Back came the query, "What has she got that I haven't?" "Nothing," replied the soldier boy, "but she has it here."

And now for the word of caution. The word here is *timeworn.* This can be as deceptive as the phrase, "practical common sense." This is the molehill behind which all too many unimaginative persons try to hide with their insecurities. Just because it was good enough for father you have no guarantee that the tried-and-true course you plan to follow is sound, simply because it comes from the musty records of yesterday. *"Time for a change,"* was a campaign slogan in recent years. I often wonder why more companies of today tend to disregard this all-important point when it comes time to evaluate the service, product, packaging, advertising, organizational policies, and the back-seat drivers who sometimes serve as executives and/or administrators.

Time to Strike It Rich

An intelligently busy person is the one who has time to get things done. This man or woman is always able to turn in a performance sheet that is inevitably noteworthy.

Why?

Simply because this individual is uniformly, and persistently, planning on how to spend that most valuable of assets—time.

My first encounter with the phrase, "plan and prosper," was imparted to me by Miss Harlow, my fourth grade teacher in the old East Vernon Grammar School in Los

Angeles. This delightful personality taught me many things which I have long remembered, but especially the value of *time*.

In a program that is designed for personal growth, it is imperative that all projects which are contemplated should be guided by the following essential points:

1. Keep it practical—or, to be blunt about it—keep your aims money-motivated. No other course of action should be tolerated.

2. Keep it positive—that is, admit nothing into your consciousness but the fully supported thought of ultimate success.

3. Keep pushing. Once you have activated a project, keep pushing hard toward your goal. Not just occasionally, but every day.

To begin with you must say "no negatives." And you must keep it that way. However, in this positive attitude of winning, let us know that you have laid the groundwork for a program of growth that is absolutely right for you and your enterprises.

Now we come to the *shocker*. All too many persons dream of becoming a millionaire, or at least comfortably affluent, but since we know that only about seven new millionaires emerge into the racing stream of commerce each and every day—and this in ratio to a population of close to two hundred million persons—we are brought up hard and short when we are forced to realize that we have encountered a *missing link* in our design for increase.

During the time this work has been in preparation, it has been necessary to query many persons on this issue and not a single individual has been fully aware of one basic fact in relation to the value of time or to what it takes to plan a successful work schedule. To be a *minute-minder* might seem to be a great bore, but let us consider this: In order to attain the status of millionaire, it is quite necessary to

put a value on the *fraction* of time we know as a *minute*.
To some, this will seem like *pennies*, but when you stop
for a moment and regard this one inescapable truth, the
minute you tend to treat so lightly is actually worth *one
dollar* in terms of present-day values. This figure multiplied by sixty adds up to sixty dollars per hour, and for a
ten-hour-day, reaches a grand total of *six hundred dollars*.
This is the money level of consciousness that you are shooting for as of this day.

Is the picture coming into focus for you now? It should,
and for the essential reason that until you do begin to put
this arbitrarily high value on each and every minute that
is in your bank account of life assets, you are not truly
thinking like a millionaire.

This increase may not come to you the first week, or even
the first year, but the essential truth is this: This plateau
of consciousness in relation to the value that you put on
your time, must be reached and sustained before real
growth can be manifested.

In clear, every-day language it means that you must plan
your work and then work your plan. This, again, might
seem to be another old-fashioned cliché, but I have some
equally good old-fashioned news for you. It works.

Translated into action, this means closely spaced appointments, carefully planned schedules, prudently and confidently planned ventures, and, above all else, a bright attitude of expectancy must pervade each of your moves.

You probably know from frustrating experience that
"The best laid schemes o' mice and men/Gang aft a-gley."
Too many time wasters will intrude. The golf-links will
beckon temptingly, or an extra smoke over a refill of coffee
will eat up precious minutes; however, when you can rise
above these obstacles you are on your way to achievement.

How to Plan Creative Rest Periods

One word of restraint is indicated. Single-mindedness of purpose is a wonderful thing, but a sense of *balance* is equally important. When the day's work schedule is complete, *relax creatively* with your family, a good book, a bit of worthy music, or any other brief indulgence of complete refreshing detachment. Once again let us revert to an old phrase, "All work and no play makes Jack a dull boy"— and in another connotation for the word *jack,* it doesn't make quite as much of this desirable increase unless these relaxing breaks are made part of the day's routine.

Good Human Relations a Must

Why learn the art and science of human relations? Because it reduces friction and increases the efficient use of time. This seems to be the greatest stumbling block for most persons who want to succeed greatly, but it can be accomplished easily. Remember, always, "a soft answer turneth away wrath." Try to find some redeeming quality in every person you meet or work with. Keep in mind that a smile, a restrained cheery greeting, a well-timed, appropriate remark (and this can be a quip, a humorous comment, or an encouraging word) often moves immovable obstacles.

How Thinking Big Improves Time Use

In the next step to riches we are going to explore the dynamic power contained within the delightful mental movement of thinking 'way beyond present capacities. On the face of it, this might appear to be a distorted view of day-dreaming, but in actual use it stretches the imagination and stimulates growth, *providing* you make notes about the plans and ideas that come to you. Later on you can sort these imaginings—like panning for gold—and by eliminating the *wild ones,* there is always the chance that you can uncover a real nugget. When you take the next step you will not only be compelled to use your time to greater advantage, but you will be riding hard toward the high plateau of great achievement.

Summary

1. Each minute of your time is worth *one dollar.* Are you preparing yourself now to collect the money that is due you?

2. Start today by being a *minute-minder* and watch your bank account, prestige, and accomplishments begin to grow.

3. One of the best ways to make the use of your minutes more efficient is to develop day-by-day, month-by-month and year-by-year plan of action, *with the emphasis on increase.*

4. The first big step is to organize yourself, then your time, and finally your plans for an orderly program of achievement.

5. Make this affirmation now with great intensity: "I know that the seven basic *uses of time* plans in action can change my life overnight."

The Eleventh Step
to Riches

How to Practice the Art of
Thinking Big

All of us are conscious of the value, even necessity, of rehearsal. We know, too, that practice makes perfect. The purpose of a repeated performance should be the attainment of perfection, regardless of whether it is a piece of music, a part in a play, or, of far greater advantage, a profit-wise venture. The skill that comes with thinking beyond one's present capacities is quite practical because this exercise is basic training for gaining great wealth.

First, you learn to think like a millionaire in the step-by-step program that is herein provided for your use, and then you learn to act like one—*in rehearsal only*—until you have acquired the riches that you are seeking.

To repeat a given series of procedures in creating a magnetic marketing program, a new and attractive package, the purchase of property, the organization of a business, the formation of a corporation, or a hundred-and-one other enterprises, there are three essential steps that must be activated, or you are courting frustration, or worse, disaster.

Learn All the Ground Rules. To accomplish this purpose

effectively you will take the subject that is presently spark-
ing your interest and learn all you can about the laws, the
procedures, the hazards, the trends, and the history, if any,
that is the essential background of the project you have in
mind. To look before you leap might be a delightful copy-
book phrase out of a McGuffey Reader, but there is one
that should be declared as equally valid in the attainment
of big money, and that is the directive: *practice before you
leap*.

The Value of a Dry Run. This means the simple expedient
of going through all of the motions of your project in mind
on paper, and then contacting the city, county, state, or
federal agencies which might be involved, or the banks,
service companies, or legal representatives that might be
part of your developing program, or idea, *without revealing your purpose*. Remember this, you aren't really thinking like a millionaire until you begin to act like one.

Now, the Dress Rehearsal. When you reach this advanced
stage of growth in your money consciousness, you will have
acquired some working capital, a broader concept of what
it means to be a millionaire, and a greatly increased reservoir of experience values. At this point in your design for
increase, you will be rehearsing for the time when you *lay
it on the line*. And this is true, regardless of whether you
are committing your money, or making a move that could
be the turning point in your life. And once again we turn
for truth to a phrase that has been greatly overworked:
"Trifles make perfection, but perfection is no trifle."

The Dynamics of Reaching

There are five tested ways by which you can give life
and vitality to your practice sessions. The only suggested

restraint is that you keep your projects within the range of probability. The reason for this is plain. The nut house is full of Napoleons now. Let's not add to the confusion that surrounds delusions of grandeur. This idea of self-discipline is offered because some of the practice moves I am going to present will seem kooky to persons as yet un-schooled in the art of thinking big for the purpose of sharp-ening the practical performance of business, or creative moves.

How to Play a Game and Start a Million Dollar Project

Years ago a parlor card game called *Pit* swept the nation. As I recall, the game was built around the operation of the Chicago grain market. Even then men, women, and chil-dren liked to think big; consequently, the contests were exciting, spirited, and, all too often, quite noisy. Some of our neighbors suggested that a good move would be some-where out in the middle of the Sahara Desert.

Later, in our own time, a new game with the name *Monopoly* burst upon the American scene. Suddenly every-body was dealing in stocks, bonds, property, and big busi-ness establishments based upon the capricious chance of the turn of a card, a roll of the dice, or a spin of the fortune wheel.

What I am suggesting is that you create your own game by the presently unlikely title of *My Million Dollars*. Only this time you will be rehearsing for the big act of your life. In your game it is suggested that you outline all of the moves, stratagems, hazards, and possibilities of the goal that you want to accomplish, and then roll dice, flip a card, or twirl a dial to see what you or your friendly opponent is to do next.

In the course of a few games you will become familiar
with all of the ordinary vagaries of fortune that might snap
at the heels of your plans, and thus you will be far better
prepared for the unexpected counter moves that could be
made against you and your projects. The reason for this is
simple. People and events are unpredictable. Consequently,
the only rational pose is one of complete preparedness.

Now we are ready for the five dynamics which I mentioned.

1. As you develop your *millionaire game,* begin to think of
yourself as a millionaire—not as a dreamer or visionary, but
in a very practical sense. This is the only way you can initiate
your program of growth.

2. Gather together all of the *positives* and *negatives* that
could possibly beset your pathway to fortune. These items of
information should include every legal, financial, practical move
or devious counter move that could be made either favorable
to or against your plan.

3. Begin to arrange the material you have collected into a
sequence of progress. The undertaking you have in mind will
have to follow certain logical procedures, starting with the very
first step provided for your use in this book, and later on,
leavened with the two final steps that are intended to give you
the all-important mental balance required to squeeze you into
the millionaire class.

4. *Find a project.* In other words, fix your interest upon a
goal, an accomplishment, a business, or a piece of property for
investment. In fact, any legitimate route to your point of attainment will serve.

5. Take a pack of 3 x 5 cards and type or write each of the
pros and cons, one to a card, until you have listed all of the
information you have uncovered about your proposed plan. My
first game took two packs of 100 cards to complete. Yours might
take less or more depending upon the project you have selected.
And don't forget to include all natural disasters, wars, mass
movements, riots, strikes, or other negative events.

Now you are ready to play the game.

You can sort your cards out according to what you think is the right way to reach your goal. You can shuffle them and pick cards at random, if this method will help your thinking. You can deal them out one at a time to yourself (and an opponent, to provide interest), or you can add the roll of a pair of dice to determine how many steps forward or backward you will take in the project you are working on—all the time trying to figure out how you can best make more progress with your plan, or how you can move in order to offset any adverse happenings.

One Man Looked Beyond the Horizon

A far-ranging genius by the name of Sanford Collins is fitting together the few remaining pieces of a project so vast that it staggers the imagination. It all started about two years ago when this venturesome man quietly acquired use rights to a rolling, rocky piece of countryside near the city of Riverside, and blandly announced that this would be the location of the 1969 California World's Fair.

Next, he requested a news conference on the site and with more guts than most embryo millionaires seem to have, went out to the property and in full view of local dignitaries, the press, and a scattered assortment of mildly interested citizens, pounded a few stakes into the ground and declared that these markers indicated where he planned to erect certain buildings, concessions, and exhibit halls.

Naturally enough, when the city fathers, prominent business men of the community, and important civic leaders managed to regain a modicum of composure, all hell broke loose. The plan was fought, denied, castigated as utterly impossible, and all but kicked out of town.

In this abnormal state of confusion, the little nearby

town of Corona took advantage of the ruckus and moved to annex the property into the city limits, and away from Riverside, where it was originally conceived.

Squeals of anguish went up from all corners of Riverside. In the meantime, Collins had moved his headquarters out of the world-famous Mission Inn to Corona. With all of this publicity, multi-millions of dollars of earnest money was pouring in from all points, including a long list of major corporations wanting in on the promotional bonanza.

This was thinking *big*, doubled and redoubled in spades.

Try it yourself sometime, provided, of course, that you have correctly prepared all of the groundwork, and implemented your grandiose scheme with all of the attributes of courage as explained for your use in Step Nine.

Why It Takes Guts to Step Into Tomorrow—Today

Some misguided persons describe this venturing into tomorrow as genius. Do not accept this term as valid. You can say that it is nothing more than raw courage, or if you prefer the less elegant term, guts. Today most persons will go along with you all the way. It is this bold attitude of daring that has made America the greatest nation on earth, despite its imperfections and the squeals of mini-brained protesters who would sell our birthright for a handout.

It is true that some of the elements which compose the special characteristics of genius derive from wanting to forge ahead of the crowd, but in the long run, it is the person with strong-willed determination who inevitably picks up all the marbles.

To Think Big—Think Big Pictures

The distinguished writer and lecturer Harold Sherman once taught me an invaluable lesson. One day we were reminiscing over coffee some of the experiences he had encountered in co-authoring with Claude Bristol the now famous book *TNT*, first published by Prentice-Hall, Inc., in 1954. "Howard," he declared with emphasis, "I have worked with business and civic groups for years, and out of my contact with these people I have reached the conclusion that persons who do not succeed greatly fail because they do not picture themselves *big enough*."

Not long after this, Sherman wrote a booklet for the Chamber of Commerce of a small town in Arkansas under the title, "Picturing Success." While the newness of this concept was upon the town there was great activity—and some progress, but after a few months the truth of his inspirational message wore off and the community slipped back into its former lethargy. All of which goes to prove one vital point: You can propel yourself into dynamic action by picturing *big* and go on to untold accomplishments by letting the Law of Inertia work for you. Unfortunately, the tendency to "remain at rest," is also part of this basic physical truth.

President Lyndon B. Johnson, early in his political career, declared to a confidant, "I have never stopped picturing myself in the White House." While it is true that he made it by a tragic twist of circumstances, it is easy to find oneself wondering if his firm, and often-pictured goal didn't set some of the powerful forces of *mind power* in motion.

While we were still in high school, Robert Knapp, later to become the well-known professor at Cal. Tech. and consulting engineer on the Manhattan Project, said to me, "I am not going to be satisfied with being just an engineer. I am going to be one of the outstanding consulting engineers in the country." At the time of his passing he had truly gained the eminence that he sought in his *big picture*.

On the day that Charles Carson, noted literary consultant, told me simply that he was going to be a writer, I am afraid that I wasn't greatly impressed, but when he went on to say, "I am not only going to be a writer, I am going to be regarded as one of the top consulting authors in the business," I knew he meant it. Those who have followed his meteoric career as I have know that he has gained his place in the literary sun.

"Thoughts Are Things"

The statement that "thoughts are things" has been repeated so often that it has reached the point of triteness, but when I first heard it from Professor Goddard back in the days when I was taking special courses in school administration, it had a solid ring of truth to me. When Goddard went on to say, "You are what you think you are," he lost me—at least for a time. It wasn't until twenty years later, when I took a course in *The Science of Mind* from Dr. Gene Emmett Clark, that the message finally penetrated my consciousness. Dr. Clark declared, "What you are thinking today will be the level of your accomplishment a year from now."

I can truthfully say that my mental regeneration began when I fully absorbed the truth of Dr. Clark's statement.

Your Ego Will Get You If You Don't Watch Out

Thinking big is a powerful attribute to nurture—providing you do it with a practical regard for the creation of a balanced personality. This concept is brought to your attention for one basic reason: *To think big is provocative, challenging, and often all too stimulating, but it must be kept under control.*

Unfortunately, the tendency is to flit off into space, with no thought of those with whom you live or work. This "ol' debbil" ego has a bad habit of joining hands with outsize dreams, with the result that the person so afflicted loses contact with reality. Your rights to a big ego, or anything else for that matter, end where the other person's begins.

Before you go on to the next vitally important step, try and assimilate this stated truth, with all of its implications. To be blunt about it, you will never be able to activate, to the full extent of its potential, the next step that is now waiting and ready for your use without this personal ego balance wheel. In fact, it is the foundation stone of the four remaining steps to a rich and rewarding life.

Summary

1. If rehearsal for success sounds like something out of bounds, try it on for size. If *practice makes perfect* for actors, musicians, or for persons engaged in competitive sports, certainly practice in the skills of thinking like a millionaire is just as important.

2. The *dry run*, or practice session, can be immensely valuable in marketing, management, land purchases, or in the planning of corporations or business enterprises. Even inventors use this technique in order to get the *subconscious mind* in gear. The hidden benefit concealed in this method derives from the fact that often flaws in thinking, or procedures, will show up startlingly clear.

3. Most persons regard the stretching and tensing of muscles for the purpose of building body vigor as a necessity, but do you make it a habit to constantly reach for the new knowledge, new skills, an expanding money consciousness, and ever greater responsibilities?

4. Start this very minute to plan and develop your own *millionaire game*. This method *in practice* will highly energize your career on the royal road to riches.

5. In learning to *think big* it helps tremendously to learn to think of yourself as a big man or big woman on campus, in business, in your profession, or on your job—and then give the big picture *substance* by outstanding performance. In order to keep this venture under control, it is suggested that you tie your ego to a lead balloon.

The Twelfth Step
to Riches

How to Get Really Steamed Up
About Something

Yes, you too, can be a millionaire. All you have to do is build a red hot fire under your aims and desires. This imagined boiling point can be triggered by most anything. It can begin with an ambition that you have secretly nurtured for years. It can erupt from a strongly motivated yen to succeed spectacularly in some field of endeavor, or spring from a spare-time hobby that suddenly reveals a potential that you hadn't previously suspected.

Then again, great fortunes have evolved from a moment of intense anger over a situation that needs to be corrected, or a new service can be imaginatively created when present facilities break down, or an invention developed that is badly needed to fill a pressing human want. Should you require more information on how best to get going, I suggest that you read my previous book, *Energizing the Twelve Powers of your Mind.*[1]

For the moment, however, here are five ways in which

[1] West Nyack, New York: Parker Publishing Company, 1966.

you can build a fire under yourself—all of them guaranteed to melt out the lead, so that you can launch yourself into the full stream of a steadily growing success.

1. First you have to isolate your motivation. Once this is determined, begin to amplify this special inducement until it reaches the boiling point.

2. It is important that you correctly evaluate your present position in terms of experience values, education, resources, money, job, environment, and locality.

3. It is quite essential that you take what you presently have to work with, regardless of how little it is and begin to grow, as of this minute.

4. Raise your consciousness of money to the million-dollar-level. If you want to, you may use the formula which I have often repeated in my writings and my lectures: "I now have all the money I want in my pocket, in the bank, or available in credit ready and waiting for my use."

5. Make a determined effort to increase your holdings of money, experience, knowledge, and skills every day, with the emphatic declaration: "Everything I do is for my growth."

How to Make the Nine Moves That Will Help You Build Intense Fire Power

In the event that none of the foregoing ideas have sparked your interest strongly enough to kick you into action, I suggest the following routines for a starter. After you have found your fire-point, go back to the five point plan just outlined for you, and then continue:

First Move. Plan a complete study of the object of your fired-up interest.

Second Move. If you are already reasonably competent in your work and your intent is to grow and expand your abilities, and speed up your progress, simply initiate a broad restudy, or research project covering the whole area of your work, trade, or profession. The purpose of this move is to locate an unsuspected treasure trove of opportunity.

Third Move. Carefully read an unabridged dictionary for words which might reveal a hidden key that could well be used in your road to discovery.

Fourth Move. Begin to make a list of all possible opportunities for increase in your probing for ideas, no matter how commonplace or far out they might seem to be.

Fifth Move. Make it a personal obligation to read at least one challenging book each week, particularly if you can find one that is related to your quest.

Sixth Move. Read all the advertising appearing in business or related trade papers or magazines. Frankly, most of them are flat and unimaginative, if not actually misleading, but occasionally a real gem will slip into the chaff and you will be off to a running start toward new areas of accomplishment.

Seventh Move. Don't be afraid to open strange doors. In practice, this means to constantly be alert to opportunities concealed in news stories. Direct inquiries to appropriate persons or firms and always enclose a stamped and self-addressed envelope.

Eighth Move. Learn to express yourself fluently and concisely. The best way I know of to accomplish this move is join your local Toastmaster or Toastmistress club. If there isn't one in your town, write to headquarters in Santa Ana, California, and find out what you have to do to get a group started.

Ninth Move. Always and everlastingly be reaching just a little beyond your present capabilities in matters of money, skills, experience-values and objectives, for this is truly the attitude of a person who is thinking like a millionaire.

How One Man Tapped a Gusher of Public Response

Should you have trouble in getting really riled up about something, I suggest that you regard for a moment the flood of response that greeted the spontaneous creation of the *Beadle Bumble Fund* by James Jackson Kilpatrick, editor of the Richmond News Leader. It seems that this worthy gentleman of the fourth estate would literally boil every time an instance of official stupidity would come to his attention. To help lessen the financial load imposed on hapless citizens, editor Kilpatrick set up the "Beadle Fund" (with apologies to Charles Dickens) for the sole purpose of meeting a crying human need. At the moment he conceived his *bright idea* he had no thought of making money, but the mere mention of the need for small donations to help the fund along brought contributions from all over the country.

At last report, editor Kilpatrick was trying to kill the idea, but inadvertently this man had tapped a gusher of human interest. The next logical step would be for some intrepid citizen to form an insurance company to help beat down the incompetent bunglers who have infiltrated our public services, as well as our elective offices. For a full explanation of the techniques required to set this concept in motion, I suggest that you go back and reread the fifth chapter of this book: Find out where the people are going and take them there.

Quite obviously, there are many instances besides quick anger or slow burning frustration that manage to conceal really big money making ideas. These plans, ideas, and outlines of new devices are often very cleverly hidden from all but the eyes of exceedingly perceptive searchers, but nonetheless they are ready and waiting for *your* use. Today!

The key to this very special quest can, of course, be fired up to the point of exploding by anger, but in this highly charged mental state there must be maintained the same attitude of a general as he observes the progress of a battle from a point of vantage and directs the movement of his troops. He must constantly be on the alert for ways and means to defeat the enemy. Here is the place where a detached viewpoint is required. A good general—and in this instance it is you—must rise above the adverse circumstance that confronts him, and find a way out. To accomplish this objective neatly, and with consummate finesse, it is necessary to have an overall picture of events in mind. Immediate questions that must be answered are these: How do I offset, circumvent, or reverse this move by my adversary? This query must be posed regardless of whether or not your opposition springs from official stupidity, a great need, a combination of circumstances beyond the control of any one person, or a violent disturbance of nature. The one thing to keep in mind is that *there is always a way out*—especially when the untoward event is met with imagination and audacity.

The Seven Additives That Must Go With the Fire Power of Anger

1. Aim right on target.
2. Know the extent of the need.
3. Like the famous Confederate general, "Get there fustest with the mostest."
4. Plan—while you are moving into confrontation.
5. Be ever ready for the unexpected.
6. Be willing to accept the inevitability of change, improvements, or direction.

7. Learn to correctly evaluate the character of the support that comes to you, especially when it is clear that you are a good six lengths ahead of your field.

How to Make the Charge of Adrenalin
Work For You

It is known that a very special hormone—adrenalin—is released by anger or excitement and tends to put real fire power into the human mechanism. I am informed and, I believe, reliably, that when this tiny drop of high-powered energy is kicked into the bloodstream, every nerve and fibre of a person's being is activated to the full extent of its present potential.

There are endless records in which mental feats of extraordinary proportions are performed, enormous weights have been lifted from loved ones, and deeds of great valor have been enacted when this extra spurt of super-charged energy is imparted to our normal capabilities. In these moments of great crisis we know the strength of ten men. It is what we do with this immense force that guides us into channels of wealth, or shunts us off into the morass of the commonplace.

Science reveals that we can discharge these special shots of energy into the bloodstream at will. All that is required is fired-up and intense

Interest
Excitement
Enthusiasm
Inspiration
Elation

-or-

Provocation

The emergency situation, of course, is always sure-fire, but we are now only concerned with normal stimulants that can propel us into the upper levels of accomplishment on demand. However, there is one word of caution that must be injected at this time: Do not overdo these self-imposed shots too often, or for any great lengths of time for the very same reason that you would not put your foot on the starter button of your car and leave it there for too long, else you would risk losing all of your battery power.

How You Can Learn to *Ride* the Rhythms of Energy

Research has proved that each of us is subject to rhythms of physical and mental energy. These rhythms swing in arcs, according to all available evidence, of anywhere from twenty-three days to as much as thirty-three days. To attempt the impossible at the lowest ebb of body or mind vigor could be disastrous, even fatal. The key to great achievement then is to first learn your physical and mental rhythms, and then be sure that, under all ordinary circumstances, you do not get riled up, or invoke these fantastic powers except at the peak of your rhythm cycle.

In addition to the cycles of high energy, there is another factor that is related in some way—how we do not know—to the time periods of high and low performance, and this is the ebb and flow of favorable circumstances. Some describe this special dispensation as luck. However, regardless of the source, or derivation, it is a part of the time cycle that must be considered. I learned long ago from the performance of others in the upper brackets of wealth and attainments that it paid off big to save up important moves for the crest of these surges of good luck to begin to build—just as the skilled surfer waits for the right wave—and then packs in every bit of action possible within the brief high-riding swell of positive energy.

In other words, and paradoxical as it might seem—if you are really thinking like a millionaire—there is a time to get steamed up about something and a time to remain cool, with everything under control.

How to Impose Self-Controls

Just as there is a right time for everything in all of our living manifestations, so there is also a time to *get mad*. You can blow your top and thus dissipate all your energies, or you can build up a head of steam and put this force to work for you in a positive manner. The choice is yours.

Some persons write letters to the editor, and when the big peeve is spelled out in bitter invective, the cause of the upset is forgotten. Some will take to the picket line, or indulge in pointless demonstrations. Some misguided individuals work themselves into such a lather that a riot is inevitable. All of these expressions are an enormous waste of energies. When the truly contemplative person takes the cause of his discontent in hand, properly evaluates his situation, and then puts some real steam behind a positive course of action, great good can accrue, not only to himself, but to all of mankind. I firmly believe it is a thought worth considering.

There are five ways which can help you harness the fantastic powers of being that are released when bitter anger strikes.

1. Slap the control valve hard and wheel right into a positive course of action. This unexpected move on your part often confounds your enemies, upsets the carefully planned steam-roller tactics of your adversary, and almost inevitably boosts you into a long head-start on your opposition because there is always a

mental *time lag* when a victim of snide backstage maneuvering, obvious skullduggery, or just plain meanness animates those who are unfriendly to your plans and purposes. Small minds always resort to these tactics, and they never seem to be prepared for a positive reaction. All other moves by a person thus put upon are anticipated, but strong affirmative responses tend to throw them off balance.

2. While the controlled anger is at its peak of power, guide this fantastic energy into channels of increase. In other words, always be prepared. What you plan need not be related to the source of your anger. In fact, it is better this way, since an overwhelming mad can easily throw you into an emotional spree with disastrous results.

3. Go on a work binge. Work day and night, if necessary, toward a positive result in order to drain off the excess energy that has been generated. If it is a way out of the calamitous event that has been forced upon you, so much the better, but vent your spleen in a manner that is profitable. Remember this: Blowing your stack hurts you alone for the plain reason that your enemy is driving hard to thwart your plans.

4. Once you are free and running clear, use this great thrust of power to reach new heights of accomplishment. Remember the Law of Inertia: *A body in motion tends to remain in motion,* and with the headstart you have achieved over the snake in the grass that has attacked you, your plans and purposes will be so enhanced that he will have difficulty in catching up with you.

5. And in final summation, don't go looking for trouble, but be prepared for any eventuality. Regardless of what you attempt or do there is a two-bit mind waiting to ensnare you, or worse, circumvent your best laid plans, for such is the stuff that, unfortunately, still animates the aboriginal instincts of primitive minds. It is a Law of the Jungle that must be reckoned with.

You will be thinking like a millionaire when you look ahead, anticipate, and be prepared for dirty pool. The next step is to have a power play ready and waiting for these distracting schemes that always seem to erupt from retarded states of consciousness.

Why Uncontrolled Anger Is Negative Emotion

While it is quite normal to become incensed over a slight, a deliberate hurt, or an outright antagonism, there is only one reaction possible from the man or woman who would increase his holdings, or add to his stature: Turn this nullifying or destructive influence into a positive, forward moving action. Any other response can destroy your health, your career, or even your life. And the very least of the harms that can come to you is the loss of days, weeks, or even months of valuable time. The trick is to control the lightning and thus guide this immense burst of energy into positive channels.

It is obvious that what I suggest takes some doing, especially in the beginning. Unfortunately, there is no ready-made harness that can be purchased for purposes of restraint. The techniques of control must be built in by you, organized by you and managed by you. There is no one, and I do mean no one, who can do this for you.

I am reminded of an effective key provided me in Stella Terrel Mann's small book, *Change Your Life Through Prayer*. This wise lady suggested, "When great bursts of anger disrupt normal mental processes, *bless* the person who is throwing the low hanging curve." With this little gambit I managed long ago to bring my fiery temper under control. I must admit, however, that in the first flush stages of using the imposed reaction, I added a four-word description of my opponent's ancestry that left no doubt in his mind as to my meaning. The big deal here is to point any built-up head of energy in the direction of success and away from disaster. You can do it, but *now is the time to begin.*

To learn the traits of character that will help you to control this lightning burst of energy is easy. All you have to do is impose a few elementary disciplines upon your explosive responses to unfriendly persons and events and you have it made. How this can be accomplished effectively will be revealed to you when you add the next step to your growing skills.

Summary

1. The foundations of many great fortunes have been laid in moments of great anger or frustration brought within manageable limits at the outset.

2. Fantastic records of accomplishment have sprung from roots nurtured by a built-in, fired-up desire to succeed. This unusual state of mind goes way beyond mere ambition because the powerful fires of desire must be started by you and the flames constantly fed by you. A little progress each and every day is essential.

3. There are nine positive moves that can be of tremendous help to you in stoking the furnace of desire. Start to build and control your fire today.

4. Learn to anticipate and correctly estimate the strength or source of trouble spots and be prepared with an offsetting plan of action.

5. Learn to ride the high rhythm waves of physical and mental energy and thus create your own good luck.

How to Achieve Maturity of Mind

The trait or characteristic we describe as maturity of mind is a many-faceted jewel. This quality not only possesses great power for enabling one to think like a millionaire, it also claims as its own a fantastic potential for attracting money, recognition and/or promotion.

How to achieve this desirable state of consciousness derives to a great extent from early experience values. If you are, or have been, a "mamma's girl" or a "mamma's boy" or an only child, you probably suffer from some type of maladjustment. This can be emotional or sexual, or you may be irresponsible or a just plain spoiled brat, regardless of your age.

How do I know? I was an only child. As I look back I shudder at the long row I had to hoe before I could even glimpse the high plateau of a mature mind.

How to Evaluate the Real You

When we reach the point in consciousness where we can look at ourselves and understand the measure of maturity, we will have taken a giant step toward achieving the "maturity concept."

In my many discussions with persons of good educational background, and with men and women who seem to be leading balanced, productive lives, I found to my astonishment on more than one occasion that this vitally important concept of looking at themselves was lacking. To find that such a situation all too often prevailed among persons with great intellectual attainment was a real shocker to me.

Look for the nine storm signals that will nearly always indicate the presence of a mind that has failed to mature, no matter how many previous accomplishments are in the record book.

Why do I ask for a serious self-examination on this point? For the very plain reason that I have witnessed all too many persons with a brilliant performance history coming unglued because of this failure to see themselves as others see them.

Your first step then is to take a long, hard look at the *real you.*

How to Overcome the Nine Obstacles to a Mature Mind

For a good, honest look at your present state of mind, ask yourself for a forthright answer to the following nine questions, and then take an even closer look at the antidote. You will then be ready to read the true story that follows. Should you see yourself in any of the stories, it is time to get busy in a hard-hitting clean-up campaign, that is, if you want to hang on to your money, or accomplishments after you have gained them.

Am I Defensive?
In other words, do I consistently shirk little responsi-

bilities or obligations, and then have to dig furiously to find some plausible explanation for my failure to deliver on time?

The Antidote

Whenever you accept an assignment, assume a liability, or take on an answerable job, get with it fast, and turn in the very best performance of which you are capable.

The Story

I once knew a salesman with a far below par record of earnings. I worked with him and I hit this point hard. From all indications this chap, whom we shall call Jack Middleton, got the message. The change-over wasn't spectacular, but there was an immediate improvement in his work. Before too long, Jack's sales equalled those of the top man in our organization, and when bonus time rolled around, he collected the largest check the company had ever paid to a field representative. Today he is salesmanager of a thriving branch office in San Francisco.

Do I Tend to Blame Others for My Failures?

I know that this is an outsize pill for most persons to swallow, but it looms large in the lives of many otherwise competent individuals. It can be the weather, other persons, or circumstances. This type of mind always has the excuse that Joe or Jane Doe is blocking his progress This one has to be watched closely because it can easily down-grade into a *persecution complex,* and we both know that the nut houses are full of men and women who have slipped into this mental quicksand.

The Antidote

In your day-to-day friction with persons and events, should you be slapped down for any reason, bounce back with all the reserve energy you can muster and resolve that the next time you will be so blankety-blank good that it won't happen again.

The Story

Many years ago I knew an executive by the name of Art Fullbright. This chap had worked himself up to a responsible post in an expanding restaurant chain. One day, and without any apparent reason other than the usual fact that a younger man could be hired for less money, he was let out. At the time Art was nearing sixty and looking forward to an early retirement. Instead of directing bitter invectives at the company, he took a close look at himself first. To say that he was devastated would be putting it mildly. He still had some bounce in him and after the initial shock had worn off, he decided to do something, but quick. Since he knew the food serving business, he bought a small, slightly-run-down cafe which possessed one saving factor—it was in a good location. Within a short time his business was flourishing . . . so much so that he soon took on a second establishment. Art is now negotiating for the purchase of the same outfit that fired him almost ten years ago.

Do I Indulge in Costly Bursts of Temper?

Temper-happy persons are forever boasting, "Boy, did I tell that guy off!" or even more asinine, "I sure let him know how I felt. . . ." This last one can be especially devastating when it is directed at a superior, an important associate, or a client. While the outburst might relieve a few inner tensions, it is like pulling the rug out from under a career.

The Antidote

Should you need to impose some restraint on your unruly temper, all you have to do is constantly remind yourself that *you* are the one who is being hurt—*you* are the one who will lose a job, a promotion, or your dream of a million dollars.

The Story

Several years ago I helped a man into a responsible position. I knew that he was well qualified for the job, and from all appearances was a level-headed, hard-working individual. What I didn't know was that he had an uncontrollable urge to blow his stack over imagined slights, or even the smallest affront to his way of thinking. His superiors put up with this immature response to persons and events for an unusually long time because of his competence, but there came a day when certain "adjustments" had to be made in the department. Naturally enough, this chap was the one who was adjusted out.

Do I Lack Self-Reliance?

To rely upon one's own ideas, acts, or abilities requires a pose of determined independence. It is unfortunate that during the centuries neither government nor religion has done much to foster this vitally important trait. However, the highest merit we ascribe to Moses, Plato, Jesus of Nazareth, Milton, and our own signers of the Declaration of Independence is that these men set small value on custom and spoke not what the mind of their day accepted as truth, but what they believed in.

It is easy to lean on someone else in commonplace things, or even in a time of great stress, but when this moment of leaning is used for more than a moment to regain needed strength, it is a costly indulgence. One who accepts more than a temporary crutch is accepting mediocrity.

The Antidote

Believe so strongly in yourself as a whole person that no man, event, or circumstance can disturb your stance of complete self-sufficiency.

The Story

In my newspapering days, I encountered a man who was having a tough go of it. At that time jobs weren't easy to come by and this chap had a family to support. He was a graduate of UCLA, with a Liberal Arts degree which didn't offer him much of a start. One day he looked his situation squarely in the face and after a soul-searching examination declared: "Since I can't get the job I want, I am going to take on the hard jobs that everybody else passes up." About the only "work" he could find was a door-to-door-commission deal selling soap powder. He reasoned that every household needed soap, so he went to work with a will. The money he earned wasn't big, but he managed to care for his small family. One day as he was canvassing he called on a lady who had a common problem. "My house needs cleaning from cellar to attic. I will buy your soap if you will take the job," she declared. He gladly accepted the work at 50¢ an hour. This wasn't much more than what he was earning in commissions, but it was a welcome change. He was determined to turn in the best kind of cleaning job of which he was capable, and he did just that. The lady was immensely pleased. She passed the word around among her friends and before too long the "cleaning man" had all the work he could manage, in fact much more. He required help. One thing led to another until one day a satisfied customer asked if he would paint his house. Again, there was added the important ingredient of giving his *best* to the job. That did it. The man in our story is now in the contracting business in a nearby foothill town, employing twelve men—four of them doing house-cleaning, and eight of them painting any structure that requires a first class job. He is making more money than he ever dreamed possible—all this because one day he decided to stand firmly on his own two feet.

Do I Have the Tendency to Think of Only the Present?

This may include family relationships, present gains, pleasures, or delights instead of long range returns. I know this one is rather extended, but it packs more power than a truck-load of TNT. All too many careers skid to a shuddering halt because of the diversions of the moment, little personal upsets, or a brief set-back in plans tend to bring on an infantile emotional response, because the person involved responded to the situation as a child would and not as a mature minded adult.

The Antidote

Train yourself to weigh the result of indulging present whims, unbridled responses, or gains against future rewards.

The Story

I once knew a man who became terribly angry with his wife over an ordinary incident in the home. In this childish emotional state, he walked out on her, leaving a completely adequate household with three promising children. He never returned. The "long and lonely road" the blues singers sing about was not music to him. He died a lonely old man twenty-seven years later in a back street rooming house in Los Angeles.

In another instance, I was well acquainted with a man in Hollywood who had advanced to a responsible executive position with a growing company. One day he worked up a rousing anger over a rough deal pulled on him by an associate and in this state of uncontrolled fury told off the president of the company for his failure to support him in the crisis. Naturally, he lost his job. From that time on, this fellow has never been more than an ordinary desk clerk. Had he controlled his childish temper, he would have gone on to great success. I thought it ironical to note that the

man who pulled the unsupportable stunt on our character
was fired two weeks after the incident for his unwise action.

Do I Show Uncontrolled Aggressiveness?

While it is true that we tend to revert to our pri-
mordial instincts as children, and tend to be aggressive to
the point of combativeness, we are not thinking like millionaires until we learn to channel this high energy potential into creative enterprises. When we learn to sublimate
the driving force of great anger and direct this power into
constructive projects, we have escaped the sticky bonds of
our aboriginal beginnings. From the vantage point of restrained and guided aggressiveness we can attain any success that pleases our fancy.

The Antidote

It has often been said that the best defense is a strong
offense. This policy might have some merit in war, religion,
and politics, but in human relations it has unusually powerful back-fire qualities, especially when the cause is less than
important. To offset this manifestation of immaturity, learn
to listen more, to share views with others rather than at-
tempting to impose them, to always make a determined
effort to find the *good* in any suggested project, plan, or
opinion, before looking for the flaws. It will work wonders
for your career.

The Story

In my early days in politics I encountered a fellow
party member who made it a point to attack everything and
everybody as a matter of principle. All motives, actions, and
decisions were suspect, and this man never spared the horses
with his biting invective. This situation prevailed regardless of whether or not he was talking to an individual or
addressing an organization meeting. Tall, lanky and lan-
tern-jawed, he was never without his big cigar. This man

had a modest but adequate sales job, owned his home, supported a good wife and two studious and well-mannered
children. This was during the worst days of the great depression when a third of the working population had no
employment. However our subject's boorishness in politics
spilled over into his home life and his wife divorced him.
With this calamity to face, he took his combativeness to
work with him, causing him to lose his job. The last time
I saw him I was shocked to see a shuffling, ragged, and un-
kempt bum heading into a skid row wine shop.

Have I Contracted the Disease of Egocentricity?

I urgently suggest that you do not pooh-pooh my idea
that egocentricity is a "disease." It is possible for a person
to become enamoured with himself like Narcissus in Greek
mythology who fell in love with his reflection in a crystal-
clear pool. In our day this tendency to nurture an over-sized
ego can be disastrous. It can so distort a person's image of
himself that he loses perspective, not only in his own capabilities, but in all his relationships with his contemporaries.

The Antidote

Should the tendency to be overly self-centered intrude into your consciousness, meet this self-love head-on
with a planned program of *sharing,* regardless of whether
this is prestige, special recognition, or an honor of some
consequence. It is always well to remember that you
wouldn't be where you are today in a civilized society if
it weren't for your associates or superiors. And it doesn't
matter if ninety-nine percent of the work, or original idea,
was yours or not. The fact still remains that *you are not the
center of the Universe.*

The Story

I know a man right now who is standing in his own
light. I dare not use his name because he is too well known

178 THE THIRTEENTH STEP TO RICHES

to the reading public. During the years, I have watched in horror as this man pulled the rug out from under himself time after time, just because he found it necessary to share a little prestige with another person. In fact, I have actually witnessed him fly all to pieces in such a situation, and then walk out on a very advantageous deal.

Are My Attitudes Toward Sex Immature?

We should learn to live with sex as mature human beings. Sex is not a toy, a cheap indulgence, or for the lack of the real thing, a colorful picture. Controlled sex can be regenerative, or uncontrolled sex can be destructive. The choice is yours.

Immature attitudes toward sex are so common that they seem to be normal. Stop at any newsstand and take a look at the magazines on display. Or, look at the advertising, and read the endless offers of erotic books, pictures, movies, even giant-size female rubber dolls that "feel just like a real, live, warm, and human woman." To pamper a taste for any one of these sex stimulants is immaturity in one of its worst manifestations.

The Antidote

Since the subject of sex is such a personal and private matter—or should be—it is impossible to plan an anonymous organization to combat this mental disease. Consequently, the only road open to any individual who honestly wants to reach new levels of consciousness is to shun all of the cheap indulgences until his problem is licked.

The Story

When I entered the craft of writing as a free-lancer, I encountered a publisher who had built a thriving business from scratch. At the time I first met this man he had several successful books on his list and his enterprise was prospering. He not only published worthwhile books, but he also managed a thriving printing business.

One day a man came to him with a filthy, but extremely profitable print job. Why the publisher took on the work I shall never know, but it seemed to release a hidden spring of interest in him. From printing the erotic junk, he was soon taking, and selling, nude pictures. In this degenerate atmosphere this man's business began to slip, slowly at first. The last time I happened to meet this man on the street he was selling printing on commission for one of his former employees. His family had abandoned him, but he was still indulging his perversion.

Do I Lack a Mature Conscience?

In all of my years of researching, I have yet to encounter a man or woman who accepted the basic principles of the Ten Commandments as a way of life who lacked a mature conscience. It is quite natural for a person living within a given cultural environment to absorb the prevailing philosophies as easily as it is for him to breathe. When the atmosphere is clear and wholesome it will naturally follow that the person will be exposed to a sound psychological growth. Unfortunately, the attitudes of our environment are not clear and wholesome—in fact, there is very little in our way of life that tends to encourage us to reach for the rewards of a fully mature mind. Just recently I queried a noted psychologist on this point and his answer was a rebuke to our way of life. According to him, "less than five percent of our people possess a mature mind."

The Antidote

Begin this very minute to examine with care your responses to people and events, your attitudes toward life, your acceptance, or rejection of sound philosophical values, and the strength of your determination to reach for the high plateaus of maturity.

The Story

During the years I have come to know a man of great

intellectual attainments, but mentally he is still a child.
His home is usually a mess, his family life is a tangle of
frustrations, his children are never reprimanded for a slam-
bang lack of consideration for others, or for an ever-increasing tendency to be destructive. From a career that
seemed to hold great promise as an educator, he keeps
slipping lower and lower on the economic scale. With a
doctorate degree in education, he is now holding down a
menial job in a nearby city, all because he couldn't stand
up to a confrontation with life.

Stop and take a very serious personal inventory. When
this is completed you will be far better prepared to take full
advantage of the next giant step toward great wealth, and
the physical reserves that are necessary to stay around long
enough to enjoy them.

Summary

1. The quality we recognize as a *mature mind* derives
from early experience values. Begin now to abandon any
childish ways left over from the growing-up process.

2. You will truly be thinking like a person who can win
and keep a million dollars when you stop and take a long,
searching and honest look at the *real you*. If you can't do
this, prepare yourself to accept mediocrity as your lot.

3. When you are taking *personal inventory* to determine
your present level of consciousness, are you operating at
the animal, average, or mature level? To reach new plateaus
of growth, I suggest you pay close attention to overcoming
the *nine obstacles* that can prevent you from gaining your
highest potential of accomplishment.

4. As you make your self-examination, be certain that
you are not handicapped by devitalizing prejudices, racial,
religious, or political, regardless of how much personal

satisfaction you get out of pampering these off-beat in-dulgences.

5. Learn to read newspapers and magazines and listen to the radio, or watch television, and still remain cool, de-tached and aloof from the blandishments of propaganda or the strongly one-sided point of view. This isn't a popu-lar attitude, but it is a step in sustaining a mature mind.

The Conservation of Body
Energies

Is uric acid really the power-packed additive that
makes a 440-volt source of super-charged energy out of a
low voltage human battery? In this instance we are talking
about the physical body that is ours.

To begin with, we should know exactly what uric acid
is. In the dictionary it is explained as a solid white substance which is only slightly soluble in water. This material
is formed in our bodies as waste matter from the complex
compound we know as protein, and can be derived from
either animal or vegetable matter although one diet fad
group insists that the product formed from vegetable matter is far less harmful to the body mechanism. It is also less
potent as a source of energy. Uric acid is probably the stuff
that puts real *zing* into the human battery.

At the present time there are numerous research projects
digging into the secrets of this lowly substance—especially
in some of the major universities. However, before you go
off on a protein binge, it might be well to wait until the
information filters down to the level of the layman through

endless examinations, cross-examinations and experimentation.

The men and women of my acquaintance who manifest a high energy potential are known to also have a high level of uric acid. Beyond this point I leave it up to the skilled technicians to determine the verities of this premise.

Should you be a person who is inclined to do a little experimenting on his own, I can only urgently suggest that you work closely with a medical doctor who is sympathetic to your venture since too much of a good thing can have unpleasant side effects.

The First Step to Top Physical Efficiency

Regardless of whether outstanding body performance can be created by uric acid, adrenalin, or some other presently unknown substance, there is one fact that we cannot deny—*unusual feats of body or mind spring from a mental climate that is strongly positive.*

Consequently, the only way to develop the greatest amount of physical efficiency, to inject real spark and enthusiasm into all of your actions so that you will always have a million pounds of forward thrust in your drive for outstanding accomplishment, is to realign the mind so that your directional force is guiding you right on target. To do this effectively, it is absolutely essential that you cleanse your mind of all frictional materials right this very minute. This assertion does not come from religion, philosophy, or ancient teachings. *It is just plain common sense.* When you have succeeded in doing this you have added a powerful ingredient to your planned program of growth.

Nine Fundamentals of Physical Power

You will truly be thinking like a millionaire, willing and able to sustain the life enrichment you are seeking when you can realistically check-chart body performance against the following basics of physical efficiency. These precepts cannot be ignored—providing, of course, that what you are planning is success-oriented, and aimed at the attainment of great wealth and/or achievement.

Regeneration. For some obscure reason, it is difficult for most persons to understand that we begin *aging* the day we are born. In order to offset this apparent paradox, it is necessary that the art, the sciences, and the skills of regeneration should be taught to children from the moment of comprehension. Included in this instruction should be certain elementary principles of physiology.

To begin with, we know that each person eats, sleeps, exercises, and indulges the act of procreation in a manner peculiar to himself. This is as it should be for in variety we can escape the commonplace. However, there are certain basic guidelines each of us must follow if we are to recoup and sustain spent body energies. To do otherwise is to invite disaster.

At this time we know that certain substances are being perfected for the purpose of extending active, fruitful years, but inherent in these energy boosters lies concealed one inescapable truth—*the miracle stimulators can only work with what you have provided.*

"What does regeneration have to do with thinking like a millionaire?" The answer is simple and direct. When any man or woman fails to think in terms of conserving the body energies, he is thinking negatively, and the mere act of indulging wasteful, even prodigal uses of our physical

resources is to risk the chance of losing the gains we are
working to attain.

Here are the remaining eight fundamentals of sustaining an efficient body mechanism. The order of presentation
isn't so important because each of the points are essential
to top performance in thinking and acting with real life
enjoyment.

Rest. To most persons this will mean eight hours of continuous sleep for each twenty-four hour period, but in
actual practice there are many deviations from this old rule.
For example, I know of one man who works and rests in a
most unusual pattern. He works four hours, sleeps soundly
for four hours, and then works for another four hours. This
routine is continuous with him, varying only if he changes
four hours of work with four hours of recreation. This
might be a game of golf, a show, dinner with friends, or a
brief motor tour to the beach or the mountains. But he
varies this schedule only slightly, and it is well to note that
his performance in the writing craft is outstanding. The
important point here is that the physical body needs time
to recharge its working batteries.

Water. To begin with, we know that this is essential to the
living process. However, very few persons realize the full
extent of this need. For example, all of us are keenly aware
of water when we are thirsty. When the need for a bath is
obvious, or when our surroundings need hosing down, or
when our clothing needs washing, we do something about
it. But few of us ever sit back for a moment and look *inside*
the body—in imagination—and regard the tremendously
vital role that water plays in activating an efficient function-
ing of the physical body. Without water, at regular intervals
during our waking hours, the fully competent use of our
mind powers and our body powers is impossible. When

water is not introduced into the body at appropriate times, some organ of our physical body suffers for this failure on our part. This is one of the four fundamental laws of nature which will not be denied.

Breath. This one is obvious, but during the years I have met so many men and women who were not operating at peak capacity because they did not know how to breathe correctly that I want to present the elementary steps so that you can really think, and act, like a millionaire.

Several years ago, I met a young man whom we will call Jack Ballard. This man was operating a small camera shop in Hollywood with only moderate success. He knew his business but every time I dropped into his shop he complained of not having enough pep to get through the day's work. Finally I suggested to him that he try deep breathing for about five minutes at least three times a day. Reluctantly, he agreed to give the idea a try.

At first his physical response was only slight, but within a few days his latent energies began to respond, and with this improvement he began to work on the idea seriously. Within two weeks he was turning out twice the volume of work, and with this increase, his business sights began to raise almost by the day. Today Jack is comfortably retired and he admits that he built up a thriving and prosperous business all because he was willing to take on extra quantities of *free fresh air* several times each day.

Nutrition. Even if you are especially interested in food, the idea of eating to live can be a dull subject. The "so-what" attitude prevails simply because the need for some kind of nourishment comes around three times a day, with monotonous regularity. The pursuit of knowledge in this field of human activity becomes interesting only when you can relate your intake of food to the success pattern you have cut out for yourself—then it takes on startling new dimensions.

First, explore the idea of *balance* in the eating process. This means a reasonably well-proportioned diet consisting of meats, vegetables, fruits and juices. To overdo on any one of these basic food items is to build up or over-activate one body organ at the expense of the other key body functions. Obviously, this unbalanced nutritional pattern can only go on just so long and *whammo!*—you have had it. All manner of upsets are just begging to take a turn at throwing you *out of gear,* and thus lessening your physical efficiency.

To offset these negatives, make a firm resolve that you will not overeat, you will not partake of one food to the exclusion of other foods *just because you like it.* The clincher on this brief guideline to better nutrition can be summed up in one power-packed sentence: chew each mouthful of food until it practically *swallows itself.*

Horace Fletcher first advocated this unusual idea back in the early days of the twentieth century, and before too long his concept became a fad, but like all other explosions of interest it languished after a few years and was soon forgotten—forgotten, that is, until later research projects in the twenties brought the healthful advantages of the plan back into general use.

The real qualities of the slow method of eating wasn't revealed until carefully controlled experiments began to disclose some previously unsuspected facts. For example, physical energies of the control group began to increase at a surprising rate, performance records in all areas of activity began to improve to a marked degree, petty illnesses were disappearing as if by magic, and most astonishing of all, the weight of the participants began to go up or down as the need of the individual required.

Sex. Carefully controlled, prudently managed sex, or sexual interest and/or indulgence can stimulate the physical body to unheard-of accomplishments, while the excessive spending of these energies, or even an overly emotional response to the idea of sex, can discharge body and mind capabilities at a fantastic rate.

The big idea is to use sex as a trigger to great achievement instead of a detonator of the atomic energies contained within the physical body. I know this regulatory attitude will demand a real effort of will, but it can be done, and the rewards are great—not only in matters of personal efficiency, but in the area of family relations, to say nothing of a tremendously enhanced skill in better management of your contacts with friends and associates, both male and female.

Exercise. Here we separate the men from the perennial playboys. In our modern world the purpose and intent of exercise should be to restore and regenerate physical energies, and definitely not the enterprise of blowing off steam to be a big man on campus, or a prodigal expenditure of physical energies just because of the mistaken idea that it is the manly thing to do. Tommyrot!

I can cite dozens of examples of the fallacy of the common "exercise belief," but one that makes the point is the restless, driving urge that compelled the late Clark Gable to be everlastingly indulging a vast expenditure of body energies. This trait was observable in him long before the tragic death of his first wife, Carole Lombard, in a plane accident while on tour of army training camps, but from then on he seemed to be insatiable in his desire to overdo. First, he joined the Air Force as a student pilot, and made the grade, rugged as it was even for younger men. He was then in his early forties, and with each new accomplishment there was yet another mountain to climb. He was planning an extremely demanding hunting trip when he was stricken—at 59—with the heart attack that took his life.

Again, exercise can be positive or negative. The positive or plus side can be achieved by the quiet, unadorned practice of isometric tensions. This means a few minutes of each day must be set aside to stretch and tense every muscle in the body. Nothing more spectacular than this, but it works wonders for the physical body. This isn't the only outstanding advantage. You will have more time for your family. You will approach your creative work with far more zest, and you will live longer and enjoy life more. Certainly this is worth lessening your participation in so-called sports that drain away your money-making potentials—and this includes long sessions on the golf links. Nine holes, maybe, but 18 or 36 not only ask for trouble, they are likely to get it.

Rhythm. This is a pattern presumed to be cosmic, that is strictly personal, and individual. No one can determine your rhythms of mental, physical or spiritual values except you. How this is managed is a subject only recently becoming a valid research project. Several recognized scientists and doctors are presently exploring this way-out guiding force, but there are some rather startling results emanating from initial experiments which are bringing to light more tentative ideas that were formerly regarded bleakly, and with no little skepticism when the concepts were first advanced in Europe. There are several books now in circulation which attempt to explain this theory, but the one, sketchy as it is, which comes the closest to shedding some light on the subject is *Biorhythm*.[1] Rhythm charts, gadgets, and full directions for determining your own rhythms are also available.

[1] New York: Crown Publishers, Inc.

Recreation. Here again we not only separate the men from the boys, but we go even farther and observe the growing, mature mind rising above the endeavors of the man or woman who has just never grown up mentally. The idea is this: *Seeds of great fortunes, outstanding accomplishments, or even the elusive goal of happiness, are nurtured in the level and extent of recreational pursuits which an individual selects for himself.*

An occasional ball game, a trip to the races, the judicious pursuit of a hobby, or an evening of restrained partying possess great value to the person indulging this brief respite from the drives of the day, but to pamper any recreational interest with more than passing attention is to weaken the whole growth pattern. To be a fan is great from the box-office point of view, but when one stops to assess the cost to himself, over and above the price of admission, the increase that he is denying himself or his family balloons to fantastic proportions.

Balanced recreational periods can provide a powerful key to the regenerative process. On the other hand, any humoring of an interest in a game or pastime of any sort, beyond casual attendance, or participation, defeats the whole purpose of body and mind renewal. The only alternative is to make the indulgence a business, money-oriented, with outstanding mastery of the game or hobby the sole objective. Then your recreational hours should turn to good books, significant plays, outstanding music, or travel that is not related in any way to the sport or activity that engages your *business* hours.

The conservation and direction of body energies is a real management job—and one that you cannot neglect for one single day. To do otherwise is far too costly in money, the attainment of goals, or your fulfillment as an eminently successful personality.

The High Potency Ingredient That Spells Success

Now that we have completed our evaluation of the first fourteen steps *in relation to our own life pattern,* the final *wrap-up* process must now be making these steps a part of our daily growth program. To leave this last, vitally potent ingredient out of our plan would be like leaving the yeast out of our bread dough—and it is how you mix and make a part of your plan of increase that will determine the quality of your leavening process as you learn to value, move toward, and thus attain the high plateau of always thinking and behaving like a millionaire.

Outstanding accomplishment is within your grasp. When you add the next and final step to your planned program of growth you've got it made.

Summary

1. The big question: Is *uric acid* the power-packed additive that puts *zing* in the human battery? If this tentative idea is true, what must be done by men of science to bring this substance into balance in the operations of the human body?

2. The first step to top physical efficiency is to know the art and skills required to *regenerate* human energies.

3. There are eight fundamentals that sustain the regenerative process: (1) Rest (2) Water (3) Breath (4) Nutrition (5) Sex (6) Exercise (7) Rhythm (8) Recreation.

4. A hobby can be restful, inspirational, money-making, or a prodigal waste of body energies. The choice is yours.

5. Good health, high physical energy, great accomplishment in any field of activity, can only spring from a mental climate that is strongly *positive.* You must now make certain that you are *success-oriented* in every respect.

How to Develop the Quality
of Decisiveness

When you hit *on target* with the right idea, and then proceed to set your bright new concept in motion, you will quickly learn that it is almost as difficult to control the flood of incoming money as it was to get it started your way in the beginning.

However, in learning to think like a millionaire, there are certain *modifiers* that inevitably come into contention: these modifiers are *other people.* This stark reality of existence must be faced with equanimity and absorbed, before too much progress can be achieved. Unfortunately there are still too many persons who operate according to the "law of the jungle," "everything and everybody is fair game for the daring," and on and on *ad nauseam,* and I wouldn't have it any other way, since this is the life blood of the competitive free enterprise system. I am fully aware that we will hear yelps of dissent from the weak, the lazy, the incompetent and the fuzzy thinking liberals, but the facts still remain the same: *We can only grow and expand with the rough-and-tumble friction of strong rivalry, regardless*

193

of whether it is honest, devious, malicious, crooked, or de-structive.

This may be a harsh estimate of our way of life, but we are not truly thinking like millionaires until we can accept these vagaries as part of our life.

I know how devastating this can be to a young man or woman just out of college, where good sportsmanship is stressed, and the competitive spirit encouraged as valid preparation for our life experiences, but we soon learn that this attitude dissolves in the operation of business, politics, religion and the professions. I know, because I have sat in the councils of all of these groups.

And again I would have it no other way, for out of such apparently negative activities we can find eventually a manner of living that will help us to gain our destiny.

The trick, or devices if we can so describe them, is for us to learn to protect ourselves *in the clinches,* for they will come just as surely as we know the sun will come up over the eastern horizon in the morning.

The first of the precepts that we must come to know intimately is the quality of decisiveness. The ability to say *yes* at the right time, and then move into action with everything we've got, or the gumption to say *no* under high pressure tactics and make our decision stick. In this latter connection it will help a lot to know that whenever a salesman begins to apply overly strong closing techniques, you must realize instantly that the good he promises is for himself and not you.

"Decisions, Decisions . . ."

Through the years a great deal of off-beat humor has been directed toward the need to make decisions. Actually, the special knack of reaching valid, and supportable conclusions comes from three easy mental movements. These are:

1. Listening.
2. Probing for facts by raising questions for discussion.
3. Sorting and evaluating the information that is gathered.

Any other procedure is sheer sophistry.

Just as there are basic qualities that reveal a person who is going places, so are there certain characteristics that conspire, in a positive manner, to make a man or woman stand out "head and shoulders" above the commonplace. These special attributes are always immediately recognizable in individuals with whom you come in contact. In fact, it is almost invariably possible to estimate a person's ability to be decisive by his appearance.

The Opposite of Decisiveness

When a man, woman or adolescent is obviously a nonconformist, bent on expressing his precious *individuality,* it is always a safe bet that he has a *scattered* mentality. The quality of decisiveness evolves only from the normal human expression. Any tendency to belittle accepted patterns of conduct simply exposes a flagrant disregard for the rights of others, obvious feelings of inferiority, and a discourtesy that is little short of primitive. In time we will come to have rehabilitation centers for this type of off-beat character.

The Five Fundamentals of Decisiveness

Now that we have the negative aspects of the ability to reach valid conclusions out of the way, let us learn the quick and easy guides to firm and purposeful resolves. Since we already know that the art and skill of making decisions that will stand up derives from listening, we will now consider the several attributes that tend to support this immensely valuable trait.

1. It has often been said that the strong feature of this special quality is a genuine pose of *crispness* in manners of speech, conduct, attitudes and conclusions.

2. A firm, long range goal of accomplishment that tends to reveal the outward characteristics of a person who is going places.

3. An individual who always seems to exemplify a positive regard for himself and his environment.

4. A person who regards progress, tempered with a high degree of discernment, supported by facts, as a way of life, and

5. The ability to view himself and the situation in which he finds himself with cool detachment.

The Story of Joe

I first knew Joe as the husband of a very promising writer. At the time he was ramrodding a live gang of grips in one of the major studios. It was well known around the lot that whenever Joe was in charge of things, lights and camera equipment would be in the right place and at the right time. His ability to make lightning decisions bordered on the fantastic.

This man always hit the deck at the precise moment set down on his call sheet, and without a moment's hesitation began to give directions to his crew in words that left no doubt as to his meaning, but the real test of his ability to make right decisions hit him one morning like a bolt out of nowhere. He had set his equipment according to plan and all of his lights were in the right place, when all of a sudden Lana Turner and the late John Hodiak developed a little hassle over who should get the favored lighting. With this kind of a temperamental situation it wasn't long until things were getting slightly out of hand. So much so, in fact, that Louis B. Mayer, directing genius of the vast studio complex, came blasting to the set with cold blue fire in his eyes. At a cost of a thousand dollars a minute I can't say that I blamed him, but in three short minutes I learned why these two men were tops in their respective jobs.

Mayer demanded of Joe, "What goes?" Most men would have crumpled under this demand from the top man but not Joe. He responded without hesitation, "We get the best all around lighting effects the way I have the lights set up." The director agreed, and Mayer snapped, "Leave it the way it is and get going." And the way he said it left no doubt in anybody's mind what he meant.

Later, during a ten-minute break I asked Joe how he could be so sure of himself with all that glamor and brass hanging on his words. "Easy," he replied, "the night before I take the time to go over the next day's shooting schedule. I review the set, the dialogue, and what the script calls for; then when I set my lights according to directions, I know I have no problem."

The moral to this story, is simply this: *"Know where you are going, and then go there."* It is as simple as that. The quality of decisiveness can only evolve from one source— *right information* correctly evaluated.

Always Expect the Unexpected—and Be Prepared

There are many ways to brace yourself for any eventuality, but probably the most unique I ever encountered was one devised by Bill Pullman, a chap I had in one of my classes in management. It seems that Bill had been thrown for a severe loss in one of his ventures, and the cause of his upset developed from a source he had least expected—a friend.

Apparently this so-called buddy was all eaten up inside over the progress that Bill was making so he pulled the plug on Bill in the most vulnerable part of his carefully laid plans. When the debris was cleared away, Bill was out of a job, and the complainer was elevated to head clerk in his department. From this point Bill kept watch of all the rat holes in any new idea that he formulated. How he accomplished this purpose bordered on the humorous at times, but his preoccupation with "what might happen," paid off handsomely for him. Here is how he did it: Whenever he took on a new project Bill would take several days to list all of the things that might upset his well laid plans. This procedure accomplished two valuable purposes. It not only spotlighted the good features of his program, but it also served to show up starkly clear any weaknesses that had been overlooked. Sometimes his list of *supposes* would grow to twenty-five or thirty items, but when Bill had completed his stand-off-and-look inventory he was a very confident man.

Throughout each day of his developing programs, he was enabled to move with deliberate speed toward his goal. As each new step in his plan of action was ready he was in a position to make his next decisive move with a boldness of spirit that brooked no challenge. Today Bill is president of his own prosperous company.

While it is unquestionably true that there is a certain magic in *thinking big,* it is equally true that the man or woman who thinks in terms of attaining great wealth always takes time to look *beyond* the obvious. On the face of it this might appear to be an unnecessary precaution, but if the *plan insurance* is good enough for smart and decisive military leaders, it is certainly good enough to be used in the highly competitive areas of *big business*. Smart strategists in the armed forces always have, complete and ready, Plan A, Plan B, and so on, until the list of possible counteractions is exhausted.

Five Ways to Sustain the Trait of Decisiveness

Regardless of whether you are buying a piece of land for an investment, a home for your family, a new car, or you are projecting yourself into the future with a carefully thought out one-year-, five-year-, or ten-year-plan, there are certain fundamentals that must be observed in each of these moves. Should you leave any one of them to chance, you are leaving a *hole in the dike* that could very easily drain off years of preparation and hard work. You can avoid this calamity by measuring your plans against this set of guidelines:

> 1. Know that "knowledge is power." When a man or woman can comprehend the one basic fact that the quality of decisiveness is founded upon *facts,* carefully collected, sorted and evaluated, the next logical step is wide open for use.

> 2. *Be an expert in something*. Regardless of what it is, when you can come to know all there is to know about one given subject, you have laid the solid rock groundwork for doing whatever you do "with neatness and dispatch."

Here's the story of Jim Knowles. Because of family prodding over his grades, Jim lost interest in school about midway through his junior year in high school, and that was it. After about three years of hard labor in the construction industry Jim began to take stock of himself. The need for more education was all too apparent, if he was going to escape the humdrum existence he had bought for himself.

When September rolled around Jim enrolled in four

classes in the adult evening school. One of the courses offered was instruction in public speaking. This interested him, even though the very idea of getting on his feet to talk in front of a group of people actually terrified him. Since his efforts to take part in the prepared speech part of the program was usually confined to a series of ums, ahs, and wells, he managed to avoid as many of the assignments as he could, but there was one part of the instruction that interested him. Why, he didn't know, but the precise rulings of parliamentary procedures snagged his attention.

Jim practically memorized the step by step processes by which formal business and legislative meetings are guided. Before too long he found himself taking an active role in this part of the class work. His fear of getting on his feet slipped away as he became more expert in the adroit use of the rules and devices employed by the *opposition* in order to circumvent the plans and purposes of his "side of the aisle." As he gained in parliamentary know-how his ability to speak in public increased steadily. As he grew in these skills he developed an interest in politics. To further his interest he registered to vote and joined the party organization of his political faith and promptly went to work with real zest. It wasn't long until Jim was recognized as a person worth watching. In the meantime his work had improved to such an extent that he advanced from a mere laborer to a minor office job in the building firm that employed him.

There came a day when the local politicians who had been left off the gravy train moved in on his employers with the obvious intent to destroy. In the publicly-aired hassle that ensued, Jim voluntarily acquitted himself so capably that the very real opposition took cover. As a result of this unexpected display of talents by a mere clerk, he was promptly promoted to contracts, and from here on his career was little short of meteoric. All because he followed his special interests and became an expert in something.

3. Obviously, the next logical step is to learn the art of public speaking—not because there is presently much need for silver-tongued orators, but for the plain reason that in the skills that must be gained in public speaking can be found the roots of decisiveness.

4. Take a course in logic. If this instruction is lacking in your community, go to the library and get a book on the subject. When this isn't possible, sign up for a course in plane geometry. The goal here is to learn the steps that produce logical thinking—and with the trait of logical thinking added to one's abilities, the characteristic of decisiveness grows and expands as an attribute in your way of doing things.

5. Learn to schedule your work. Plan all of your activities in the most efficient manner. Review the Tenth Step covering the use of time, page 135.

Find an Economic Need and Fill It

In no other country in this crazy mixed-up world, and at no other time in the vagrant history of man, have the chances of becoming a millionaire been so good, or the trend of events offered so many opportunities to gain great wealth. It is fantastic.

There is very little in this world that does not respond to a definiteness of purpose. And this one powerful additive to the total personality tends to impart an aura of preciseness, *in a manner that can be acquired in no other way.*

Actually, when you get right down to basic cause, purpose is the first common denominator in the search for success. When the fact of determined intent is included in the human expression—and at this moment we are think-

ing of yours in particular, there is no place else to go but
up. With this priceless ingredient made a part of your
planned program of growth, the next step is to find a need
in a category of activity and fill it, with imagination, tempered only with a decent regard for the practical aspects
of your innovation.

Within the week, three way-out plans and devices that
are making their creators wealthy have come to my attention. The first one was a newly developed electronic com-
puter system that will eliminate the need to carry cash for
any purpose. The initial tryout of this service will be in
the giant California World's Fair that will be staged right
here in Riverside. The idea of electronic currency may be
nationwide by the time this book is released. The inventor,
Dr. Melvin E. Salveson, claims many exciting uses will be
made of his brain child, but I can see very clearly that the
days of pickpockets, holdup men and bank robbers are
numbered by this device.

In another instance, a two-point combination lock on
the dashboard of a car—a simple device that can be in-
stalled quite inexpensively at the factory, can reduce car
thefts almost to zero. The big idea here is that when the
ignition is turned off, the only way the car can again be
started is for the driver to dial to points 1 and 2, with the
sequence of numbers known only to himself, before his
key can start the motor.

With the third example the privacy of the bathroom has
been invaded. This time by a device by the unlikely name
of Bidet, pronounced bee-day. This contraption eliminates
the use of toilet paper and substitutes a fast wash and dry
system. The small appliance can be attached in minutes to
any ordinary toilet seat and plugged into the nearest elec-
trical outlet. Many unusual claims are made for the gadget,

but perhaps the most startling is the way it is supposed to perform the quick and sanitary functions of feminine hygiene.

Quite obviously the persons who have perfected these ideas have created something far more important. For example, new protections, services and convenience have been added to our way of life, productive wealth has been achieved, simply by creating more jobs, and with this advance, the purchasing power of many individuals has been greatly increased.

With this growth in earning potential pushing at the overstretched seams of our economy, it should be obvious to any thinking person that we are confronted with opportunities unlimited. Especially when you take a moment to contemplate the fact that the three ideas I have just described are repeated in different ways on an average of 5600 times each year, and that these basic devices and plans are again multiplied at least seven times the following year, I often wonder why anyone with an ounce of guts can avoid being hit with a million-dollar enterprise.

During the two years that I collected material for this book my own eyes have been opened so wide that I am completely flabbergasted. So many available ideas, plans and devices have come to my attention that I sometimes feel as if I have a private key to the treasure vaults of the world. The only restraining influence is the simple fact that at my time of life I am doing the one thing I have always wanted to do, and that, after all, is accomplishment enough, but you—with ten, twenty, or even forty productive years ahead of you—should take a headlong dive into a rich and rewarding future, overflowing with wealth, achievement, or the personal satisfaction of service to mankind. As of today the choice is yours.

Summary

1. We can only grow and expand in body, mind, and spirit with the rough and tumble fiction of strong rivalry, regardless of whether it is positive (with us) or negative (against us). The strategy here is to learn to ride with it (good human relations) or be prepared to meet the devious, malicious, or crooked attacks of the twisted mentality.

2. The first steps to the art and skill of decision making can be gained by absorbing an easily learned formula:

    a. Listening
    b. Probing
    c. Sorting and evaluating information that is gathered.

3. The fundamentals of the quality of decisiveness can be acquired very quickly by:

    a. Developing an attitude of crispness in manners of speech, conduct, attitudes and conclusions.
    b. Establishing long range goals of accomplishment.
    c. A firm and positive belief in yourself and your environment.
    d. Having a high regard for practical progress.
    e. By developing the ability to evaluate yourself realistically.

4. Always expect the unexpected, and be prepared with plans adequate to meet the emergency.

5. The knack of sustaining the quality of decisiveness can be greatly increased by these rules:

    a. Never be satisfied with anything less than the full facts in any situation.
    b. Resolve to be an expert in something.
    c. Learn to express yourself clearly and forcefully.
    d Train yourself to think logically, or with *continuity*.
    e. Learn to schedule your work, your plans and activities. *In other words, think and plan ahead.*